T0160535

SOLD

# SOLD

Every real estate agent's guide to building a profitable business

**BY DAVID GREENE**

BiggerPockets®
PUBLISHING
Denver, Colorado

# *Praise for*
# SOLD

---

"As the person who brought David into real estate sales, I've watched his growth in this area from zero to hero. David's explanations and systems for how to become a top-producing agent are unquestionably effective. I can't think of a better person to write a book this needed in the industry."

**—David Osborn, *New York Times* bestselling author of *Wealth Can't Wait* and *Bidding to Buy***

"David opens up his entire playbook here and doesn't leave anything out. A must-have for any agent who takes their business seriously."

**—Aaron Amuchastegui, host of Real Estate Rockstars podcast and author of *Bidding to Buy***

"I wish this book had existed when I was selling real estate! David has done a fantastic job of breaking down what it takes to be successful into simple, easy-to-follow steps that help agents master their craft and become top producers. I love this book!"

**—Pat Hiban, former No. 1 agent for both Keller Williams and Re/Max, *New York Times* bestselling author of *6 Steps to 7 Figures***

This publication is protected under the U.S. Copyright Act of 1976 and all other applicable international, federal, state, and local laws, and all rights are reserved, including resale rights: You are not allowed to reproduce, transmit, or sell this book in part or in full without the written permission of the publisher.

**Limit of Liability:** Although the author and publisher have made reasonable efforts to ensure that the contents of this book were correct at press time, the author and publisher do not make, and hereby disclaim, any representations and warranties regarding the content of the book, whether express or implied, including implied warranties of merchantability or fitness for a particular purpose. You use the contents in this book at your own risk. Author and publisher hereby disclaim any liability to any other party for any loss, damage, or cost arising from or related to the accuracy or completeness of the contents of the book, including any errors or omissions in this book, regardless of the cause. Neither the author nor the publisher shall be held liable or responsible to any person or entity with respect to any loss or incidental, indirect, or consequential damages caused, or alleged to have been caused, directly or indirectly, by the contents contained herein. The contents of this book are informational in nature and are not legal or tax advice, and the authors and publishers are not engaged in the provision of legal, tax or any other advice. You should seek your own advice from professional advisors, including lawyers and accountants, regarding the legal, tax, and financial implications of any real estate transaction you contemplate.

**SOLD: Every Real Estate Agent's Guide to Building a Profitable Business**
David Greene

**Published by BiggerPockets Publishing LLC, Denver, CO**
Copyright © 2020 by David Greene.
All Rights Reserved.

Publisher's Cataloging-in-Publication Data

Names: Greene, David M., author.

Title: Sold : every real estate agent's guide to building a profitable business / by David Greene.

Series: Top-Producing Real Estate Agent

Description: Includes bibliographical references. | Denver, CO: BiggerPockets Publishing, 2020.

Identifiers: LCCN: 2020941714 | ISBN: 9781947200371 (pbk.) | 9781947200388 (ebook)

Subjects: LCSH Real estate business--United States. | Real estate agents--United States. | Success in business--United States. | BISAC BUSINESS & ECONOMICS / Real Estate / General | BUSINESS & ECONOMICS / Real Estate / Buying & Selling Homes | BUSINESS & ECONOMICS / Sales & Selling / General

Classification: LCC HD1375 .G691 2021 | DDC 333.33/068/8--dc23

**Printed on recycled paper in the United States of America**
10  9  8  7  6  5  4  3  2

# TABLE OF CONTENTS

## CHAPTER SIX
# LEAD FOLLOW-UP

## CHAPTER SEVEN
# THE FUNDAMENTALS OF REAL ESTATE SALES

**CHAPTER** > **ONE**

# INTRODUCTION

S tatistics show that nearly 87 percent of new real estate agents quit within their first year. What a number! Why do so many agents fail or quit so quickly? My aim in writing this book is to help you answer that question and help you *not become just another statistic.* Well, I do want you to become a statistic, but just the kind that wins—that precious 13 percent of new agents.

First rule? It's all about your mindset. Since most of us had other jobs before becoming licensed agents, we may carry preconceived beliefs into the profession based on our earlier experiences. While it makes sense to assume what we learned at previous jobs would be applicable to this new field, that's not always the case.

Agents need to be many things all at once. At times you will wear the hats of legal counsel, therapist, financial advisor, friend, organizer, market expert, and salesperson. Odds are the hats you are most comfortable wearing are the same hats you wore in previous occupations. We tend to build upon our past success, using those previous experiences as building blocks to help us achieve new heights.

However, our previous experiences can also hold us back. Self-limiting beliefs, unreasonable expectations, or a reluctance to accept and adapt to our new environment can hurt our chances for success. Having worked with dozens of new agents on my own team, coached dozens more, and trained hundreds, I believe the No. 1 reason most do not find real estate as exciting or lucrative as they hoped is because they try to apply their past experiences to their new environment. I believe this is a problem throughout our society.

Consider our public school system. Children are told when to arrive for class, where to sit, what to study, and when they will be tested. Their daily schedule is orchestrated by a bell that rings at predetermined times. Their performance is graded on a five-point system, and they are allowed to progress through the school system as long as they meet the minimum standards. They are evaluated based on tests that primarily measure their ability to recall information based on memorization. Unfortunately, students are not taught how to *learn*, and do not develop the skills required to navigate life outside of school. As a result, students are not prepared to succeed in today's workforce.

The public school system and the model it follows are not evil. They were created during the Industrial Revolution, when factories needed employees who could stand on an assembly line or operate a piece of machinery for significant periods of time without losing focus. Today's workplace requires a different set of skills, which the students' education has not provided. Problems arise when those students are then dropped into a work environment for which they have not been properly prepared. Those who take longer to adapt to this new environment may find themselves out of a job. Those who *do* adapt may find the process difficult and confusing.

As an agent who is entering the world of real estate sales, you are being dropped into an environment that is completely different from anything else you've ever experienced. If you aren't prepared for what to expect and don't adapt quickly, you will find yourself frustrated, discouraged, and ultimately hopeless. The faster you can adapt, the faster you can start generating revenue.

## What No One Tells New Agents

A new agent needs to understand that no one will be sending them clients. In general, real estate agents are required to find their own. Even those who join a team will still be expected to make a huge effort to find their own clients. This effort is referred to as lead generation, the single most important thing an agent can do to generate revenue.

However, most agents hate lead generation and will do anything to avoid it. If you happen to be one of the few who enjoy it, count your lucky stars as you're already at a huge advantage over your competition. Many agents say they hate lead generation due to fear of rejection and discomfort with asking people directly for their business. It can feel pushy, selfish, and greedy. I don't believe these are the real reasons agents don't like lead generation. I've seen enough agents ask for business in a completely natural way to understand that it doesn't have to feel awkward.

I believe the real reason new agents don't like lead generation is because they've never done it before, and nobody has told them it is essential to success in real estate sales. When you get your real estate license, you are essentially receiving nothing more than the right to earn a commission by representing a buyer or a seller on the purchase or sale of a house. This right is valuable to you only if you find a way to put it to use. New agents often mistakenly believe that getting their license is the functional equivalent of getting a job. It's not! Jobs pay you for showing up. Owning a business pays only when you find customers. The real estate agents who figure this out the quickest tend to get off to a fast start in the industry.

## The Math to $100,000

Working as an employee typically involves following policies and procedures someone else has already developed, and largely ignoring any aspect of the business you aren't directly responsible for. It is rarely essential that an employee understand the numbers side of running a profitable business. But if you want to adjust to the world of sales, you should understand the math involved in earning a paycheck.

When I interview agents who want to join my team, I always ask them how much money they would like to make in their first year. Almost all of them say the same thing: $100,000. Something about that number just appeals to people.

It is entirely possible to make $100,000 in your first year (though how difficult it will be depends on the price of homes in your area). I'm going to break down the math to show you how. I assume you will follow the advice in this book, and average one seller closing and one buyer closing each month. Below are the assumptions I've used to run the numbers.

**Expenses:**
- Annual commission cap (money paid to the broker): $15,000
- Annual expenses: $35,000
- Gross expenses: $50,000 ($35,000 expenses + $15,000 cap)

**Seller closings:**
- Average purchase price: $250,000
- Average commission: 3% ($7,500)
- Twelve sellers = $90,000 ($7,500 x 12)

**Buyer closings:**
- Average price: $250,000
- Average commission: 2.5% ($6,250)
- Twelve buyers = $75,000 ($6,250 x 12)

If you complete twelve buyer closings a year, you can expect to make $75,000 in gross commission. If you add twelve seller closings a year, you can expect to make an additional $90,000. That equals $165,000 a year. After subtracting annual expenses of $50,000, you are left with a net profit of $115,000.

Now let's work backward to come up with a system that will lead to this $115,000. According to *The Millionaire Real Estate Agent* by Gary Keller (with Dave Jenks and Jay Papasan), for every twelve people in your database whom you contact thirty-three times in a year, you can expect to receive two referrals a year. We are going to assume it is your first year and your skills are lacking, so it will take twice as many people in your database to get the same result (twenty-four people to receive two referrals). We will also assume those two referrals consist of one buyer and one seller. From a very general perspective, your simplified system will look like this:

- Assuming a 50 percent success rate, twelve closed sellers a year will require twenty-four seller appointments per year
- Twenty-four appointments per year will require 288 people in your database (288 ÷ 12 = 24 appointments)
- Twenty-four appointments per year = two appointments per month
- Two appointments per month at a 50 percent success rate = one closed seller per month

Now let's look at the math for buyers:
- Assuming a 50 percent success rate, twelve closed buyers a year will require twenty-four buyer appointments per year
- Twenty-four appointments per year will require 288 people in your database (288 ÷ 12 = 24 appointments)
- Twenty-four appointments per year = two appointments per month
- Two appointments per month at a 50 percent success rate = one closed buyer per month

To sum up: If we combine buyer and seller closings and assume a 50 percent success rate, we can see that closing one buyer and one seller per month will require 288 people in our database whom we meet and communicate with approximately three times per month (thirty-three times per year).

As you can see, building and maintaining a solid database is the most important thing you can do to ensure a steady stream of client referrals. Top-producing agents excel at this. Not only can you make more than $100,000 a year by locking in one seller and one buyer closing a month, but if you then add in the new lead-generation strategies I will share with you, you could even make more than $200,000 a year as a real estate agent.

## Why Most Agents Don't Succeed

As a licensed real estate agent, you don't work a job—you own a business. There is a big difference between the two. If you bring a job mentality to a owning a business, you will find yourself confused and frustrated.

| JOB | BUSINESS |
|---|---|
| Requires you to show up and work a set schedule | Requires you to work whenever there is work that needs to be done |
| Provides steady income that is often unrelated to your performance | Provides income that is not steady but is directly related to your performance |
| Allows you to focus solely on the specific task or role you were hired to do | Forces you to learn and succeed at every role and task that you have not hired someone else to do |

| Removes responsibility for the outcome from you | Places responsibility for the outcome on you |
| --- | --- |
| Allows you to focus on your personal needs | Forces you to focus on the needs of the business |
| Usually provides customers for you to service | Requires you to find customers to service |

That last difference is where most new agents experience culture shock. Nearly every job most of us had before becoming a real estate agent involved someone else finding customers for us to service. When we bring this mindset into our new business, we are set up to fail. Owning a real estate business is like working as a server in a restaurant. You must know the menu (the market), make solid recommendations (advise on the right house or the right list price), communicate with the kitchen (lenders, title, escrow companies, etc.), coordinate the delivery of the food (manage your escrow timelines), and keep your customers happy and satisfied throughout the dining experience (buying or selling process).

The one big difference is that in a restaurant, customers are brought directly to your table. Owning a real estate business is like a being a server who's required to go find customers and then convince them to come eat at your table! This requires skills many of us haven't developed. We are comfortable serving the customer, but finding them, convincing them, and then closing the sale requires a completely different skill set. Once you understand this, you'll be on your way to adopting the mindset you'll need to become a successful agent.

When you first enter the world of real estate sales, you may encounter little support, insufficient training, and the uncomfortable feeling that you are on your own. Perhaps you've already experienced this and that's why you're reading this book.

The purpose of this book is to provide you with what no one else will— and what no one provided me. It contains the questions you should be asking and, when possible, the answers to those questions. It will help you shift your thinking and adapt to this new world. Your ability to do so will ultimately determine whether you thrive or barely survive in the competitive, creative, and wildly adventurous world of real estate sales.

Sound tough? It's not all bad. Owning a business has its perks too. For one, there is nobody to stop you from reaching your maximum potential.

You'll also find it can be incredibly addicting to blur the lines between work and leisure. Getting paid to vacation with friends, attend parties, and build authentic relationships isn't a bad way to make a living. In general, the more well-respected you are within your community, the more likely you are to get additional clients. Getting paid to be likable and show up as someone's guide is pretty nice too. If you enjoy freedom, autonomy, and limitless potential, you may love this business.

Another advantage to working in real estate sales is the wealth of information and training you can find. Some of the best speakers and brightest minds in the world provide sales training to agents. Do you enjoy knowing you have complete control over your own success, income, and work schedule? Then owning a real estate business is a great place for you to be.

My favorite aspect of the business is the amount of personal growth required to succeed. New agents often start off thinking they need more industry knowledge to get ahead, but I've found this is rarely the case. Most of the time the solutions to the problems we encounter are psychological, not tactical, in nature. Your ability to grow as a person, a communicator, and an entrepreneur will dictate your professional growth.

The agents who do best in this business are those who treat their business like it's a business. If you treat your business like a hobby, your clients will pick up on that and your results will reflect it.

Treating your business like a business means treating your profession and your clients with the respect they deserve. It means giving your best every day and understanding that the better you do your job, the more money you can save or make for your clients, which in turn allows them to endure less stress. You should arrive at your office expecting a client to call and want to meet with you. Dress accordingly. Understand that simply showing up at the office won't get you paid. It's what you do while you're there that matters.

## Common Mindset Mistakes

Several other challenges unique to real estate sales can sabotage your odds for success if you aren't prepared for them. Let's explore some other misconceptions that are common among newer agents.

## Being at the Office Will Make Me Money

Most jobs do not compensate employees based on their productivity. Instead, employees must meet certain minimum standards in order to keep their job, and compensation is based on the hours they are on the clock. This creates a mindset that equates productivity to hours spent at the workplace.

In the world of real estate sales, this mindset is counterintuitive. I cannot tell you how many times I walk through the office and see cubicles full of agents talking to each other. In fact, the office is filled with distractions, and it's your job to make sure you avoid them. You'll rarely find business by talking to your competition. If you want to make money, you've got to stay productive. If you want to be productive, you've got to focus on income-generating activities. Simply being in the office will not make you money!

In fact, being in the office *costs* you money. To stay in business, I must pay for office space, utilities, access to the Multiple Listing Service (MLS), software subscriptions, business clothing, error and omissions insurance, and a host of other items. Every day I am in the office, I am forced to spend money for the right to hold a license that allows me to earn a commission. Being reminded of this helps me stay focused on the importance of finding my next client and keeps my priorities in order.

## If I'm Staying Busy, I'm Being Productive

Many things will cross your desk in a day: emails from vendors, title companies, and other agents; inquiries on properties from hot leads (or not-so-hot leads); compliance messages; reminders; and sales pitches from marketing companies. The hours in a workday are finite. Nobody else is going to help you decide what is worthy of your time and what is not.

If you want to avoid wasting time on things that will not earn you money, it's your job to make that happen. Now that you own your own business, you must learn to identify which projects have the potential to generate revenue and which do not. You'll have to set priorities.

## I Can Rely on Others to Train Me

In most jobs, you are assigned someone to train you when you first start. This is usually an experienced employee who is being paid to teach you how to do the same things they do for the company. If this has been your experience, you might be expecting someone else to guide you or act as a sort of mentor. That would be a big mistake.

As a real estate agent, you are an independent contractor who holds their license under the supervision of a broker. While most brokers do offer some kind of training, I have yet to meet the agent who was actually content with the training their broker provided them. Assume right now that you will be disappointed with the level of training you receive. It is your responsibility to learn everything you need to know in order to succeed in this job. The less you expect others to show you what to do, the better your attitude will be and the quicker you'll pick things up. If you want someone else to care about your business, you'll need to create those alliances on your own.

The acronym PLAN will help you quickly determine whether or not something has the potential to generate revenue. PLAN stands for:

- Prospect
- Lead follow-up
- Appointments
- Negotiate

These four activities will net you the highest return on your time. Learning to push aside, leverage away, or turn down work and opportunities that do not fall into these categories will help you remain in revenue-producing mode.

## I Don't Really Need to Generate Sales

As a salesperson you are always, *always* looking for your next client. There is a common concept called "always working, never working" that speaks to developing a mindset in which you are consistently generating leads and looking for new revenue while still living a fulfilling life. A real estate agent is many things—so many, in fact, that it's easy to forget your first priority, which will always be to generate sales. Agents who forget this usually don't last long. Be aware of how easy it is to be seduced away from always looking for your next client, and make sure this never happens to you.

First off, sales isn't for everyone. Asking for business, risking rejection, and accepting the fact that you need to work your career into the other areas of your life can be a tough pill to swallow. Second, aspects of the career are very rewarding. You get to be involved in the biggest, and sometimes scariest, purchase that most people will ever make in their lives. You will often be considered a guide, confidant, expert, therapist, and possibly even a lifelong friend. The emotional gratification the career provides can be intoxicating.

Be careful to use this emotional paycheck as fuel to continue *pursuing* sales activities, not to replace them. It's all too easy to neglect the physical paycheck that requires work you don't enjoy. If this happens, you may find yourself unable to generate the emotional paycheck you've come to love when the physical paychecks stop coming.

To avoid this, you'll use the tools of the sales funnel to keep clients moving along the path from prospect to paycheck. The better you become with your tools, the more clients you will help. If you chase excellence in your craft through mastery of your tools, you will earn a physical paycheck as well as an emotional one. If you pursue only the emotional paycheck, you'll eventually be left with neither.

## If I Go to the Office Today, I'll Be Successful

In most life situations, a sense of urgency is frowned upon. It often leads to mistakes, impatience, and rushed decisions that don't always work out. But in real estate sales a sense of urgency can be a useful tool, and you'll be relying on it to help your clients deal with stressful situations.

As a police officer, I often experienced a sense of urgency. Several times throughout a shift I would be dropped into challenging situations. Time was rarely on my side. I frequently found myself forced to make a decision with limited information, unsure of how that decision would impact the long string of unseen dominoes likely to be set in motion by it. I had to make peace with the fact that there were too many variables for any human mind to reasonably consider and make the best decision I could in the moment.

When new officers were faced with too many variables to absorb at one time, they would typically do what almost everyone does in such moments—freeze. Whenever I would see a fellow officer freeze, I would help snap them out of it by creating a sense of urgency. "Hurry, cut them off at Fourth Street!" or "Tell dispatch what that witness just said, and I'll grab the car!"

My assuredness in making a decision coupled with the sense of urgency in my voice were enough to get my partners moving again. You will have to play this role with your clients. They will be relying on their emotions to make decisions, and those emotions will be swinging wildly. It's your job to help regulate your clients' rapidly fluctuating emotions. Being able to create a sense of urgency is one of the most important tools at your disposal for doing so.

In times of uncertainty, when we find ourselves paralyzed, we are most likely to turn to someone else for help—especially if that person exudes confidence. *You* are that person for your clients, and your sense of urgency can be the perfect prescription to free them from paralysis. Creating a sense of urgency for clients can be uncomfortable and may even feel wrong—especially if you are a people pleaser. Keep in mind that you're doing it only to help your clients when they need your help most.

## I'm in Real Estate Sales—I Don't Need to Worry About Accounting

Unless you were an accountant in your previous career, you probably didn't need to look at your company's profit and loss statement (P&L). As a business owner, you are now responsible for not only making sure your business is profitable but also tracking your revenue and expenses. By doing this, you'll know how profitable you are and what types of adjustments you should make to run your business better.

You'll want to find yourself a competent certified public accountant (CPA) sooner rather than later. A good CPA will make sure you start taking advantage of every deduction you can, then work backward to find tax-deductible activities you can use to generate new business for yourself while also enjoying your life. Dinners, trips, clothes, your phone, even your vehicle can be written off when done properly. Remember, you will also be responsible for setting aside a portion of your income to pay your federal and state taxes. Now that you're an independent contractor, it's easy to think the whole paycheck is yours. It's not! Uncle Sam will still want a piece of the pie.

## Now That I'm Self-Employed, I No Longer Have a Boss

Many real estate agents who come to the profession from a W-2 job think they've escaped having a boss and can do anything they want. This could not be further from the truth. New agents don't trade in one boss for no boss—they trade in one boss for many bosses. In fact, the whole goal of becoming a top producer is to get as many bosses as you can. Your clients become your boss when you sign up to work for them. Those clients will play a huge role in dictating the experience you have in the industry, and your ability to work successfully with them will play a large role in the quality of your life.

My team strives to have thirty bosses at any given time: We want thirty houses in escrow on average. I understand that I work for others and the more bosses I have, the more money I make. Top-producing agents have made peace with the fact that they have many bosses.

# KEY CHAPTER POINTS

- Your mindset is the first thing you must change in order to become a top-producing agent. Shifting your thinking from "employee" to "business owner" is crucial.
- Employees worry only about themselves and their own role within the company. Business owners must worry about every role.
- You probably think like an employee because you were conditioned to, through no fault of your own.
- Your first priority is to find new clients. This is unlike most jobs, where the employer provides the client and the employee services them.
- You can make $100,000 in your first year as a real estate agent if you sell one listing and close one buyer (at an average price point of $250,000) a month.
- You can be in the office all day and do no work.
- Learning how to prioritize the types of tasks that cross your path each workday is crucial to your success.
- Follow PLAN (prospect, lead follow-up, appointments, negotiate) to stay focused on revenue-generating activities.
- Forgetting you are in sales can lead to losing your business entirely.
- Creating a sense of urgency can be an effective tool for helping clients make decisions.
- Learning to track revenue and expenses is your job as a business owner, and a CPA can be a big help with that.

**TWO**

# NEW AGENT QUESTIONS

A s a new agent in the office you are *sure* to have a list of questions you need answered. Even if you're an experienced agent, you may still be walking around feeling that you don't know exactly what you're doing. This is normal. In most of our previous jobs, we were trained on how to perform our duties correctly before being unleashed on customers. Real estate sales is unique because you are an independent contractor and must learn as you go.

If you want to be effective at generating leads, you've got to project assertiveness and confidence. To do so, you must have a strong grasp of the duties the job requires and how to perform them correctly. This chapter is intended to help you learn exactly that. I'm going to answer most of the questions new agents have when starting out that their brokers may be too busy, or simply not interested enough, to answer. By the time you've finished reading this chapter, you should feel more confident in your ability to fit into the culture of the real estate world.

## New Agent Intimidation

First off, every new agent is going to feel intimidated. We all experience this, but it doesn't go away with time—it goes away with experience. You can be in the business for three years, but if you don't sell a house, or sell only a couple, you're still going to feel like a new agent. Many agents never get over this feeling, and it can be especially difficult for those who are older than their peers or start their real estate career later in life. Being intimidated can keep you from making progress since you lack the confidence to take the actions required to grow in knowledge and experience.

You will often hear other agents in the office using terminology you are unfamiliar with. This can make you feel like you don't belong, and you might be afraid to ask them what they really mean. In fact, you probably understand exactly what they are talking about—you just aren't familiar with their jargon. That's why I've dedicated a section of this chapter to explaining real estate agent terminology.

You may also feel uncomfortable speaking to other real estate agents because you aren't quite sure what you're "supposed" to be saying. The same goes for speaking with clients, especially if you've never sold a house. I'll cover those concerns in this chapter as well.

The bottom line is that you don't want to let new agent intimidation stop you from taking the action you need to learn the business and excel at real estate sales. Everyone else was new at one point, and we all remember what it was like. Most other agents won't judge you as harshly as you might expect—unless you pretend to know more than you do and get caught. That's how ego can definitely hold you back. Instead, accept that you have a lot to learn; this will help you feel more comfortable and prepare you to absorb new information.

The fastest way to gain confidence is to learn the fundamentals of what you'll be doing. (There's a chapter dedicated to that too.) As you read through this book, try to imagine yourself explaining these concepts to another new agent who came in right behind you. Studies show that if you learn while intending to teach someone else, your brain retains more information than with any other method. Teaching others will help you develop not just a firm grasp of the information but also confidence, which will replace the intimidation most new agents experience.

## Choosing a Broker

*How do I select the right broker for me?* Although this is the first question nearly every new real estate agent asks, I believe which broker you choose will have a very small impact on your overall success. In fact, it can be one of the least important decisions you'll have to make.

No matter whom you choose, you will likely be disappointed. Brokers simply cannot meet most new agents' expectations when it comes to offering training, alleviating anxiety, and providing opportunity. While agents know they will be independent contractors, they rarely understand what that means. In essence, being an independent contractor means you're on your own.

Brokers are in the business of recruiting agents. The more agents in their company, and the more those agents sell, the more money the broker makes. This means brokers have two main goals:

1. Recruit more agents.
2. Keep their top producers happy and productive.

If you are a top-producing agent, you will get more attention, resources, and support than other agents. This may seem unfair, but it's really quite fair. The agents who generate the most income for their brokers are the ones who keep the lights on and the bills paid. They have earned the right to their broker's support. As a new agent, you have not, even though you may actually need it the most.

That's why I warn new agents that they will be disappointed with any broker they choose. The problem is exacerbated by the fact that a broker's first job is to recruit new agents. Guess how they do that? By promising them great training, great support, and great systems. Unkept promises are a recipe for disappointment.

Nonetheless, you will still have to select a broker, and there are several types to choose from. Each has their own unique set of value propositions, commission splits, support services, and training. Your best bet is to choose the brokerage that makes the most sense for your personality.

## A History of Brokers

To understand why you need to select a broker in the first place, you should understand what a broker actually does for you, and how the broker's role came to be what it is today. A salesperson cannot be compensated for the sale of a property—only a broker can. When you take a listing to sell a property, it is actually your broker who is taking the listing. Your broker then authorizes you, the salesperson, to represent the brokerage in communicating with the client to facilitate the sale. The same is true for buyers.

Originally, brokers performed all real estate transactions. They would take listings and market them only to buyers who came to *their specific brokerage*. Each broker would have a book, or list, of their "listings" and would show them to the buyers who came to look at them. If Broker A did not have a home for sale that you liked, you would go check out the properties Broker B was offering. If a broker wanted to make sure you looked only at their listings, they would have you sign a buyer-broker agreement, meaning you could buy a home only from their brokerage.

At a certain point, brokers realized it did not make sense to show buyers only their own listings. Buyers were hesitant to commit to smaller brokerages that had fewer listings. The big companies were taking all the business, so the little ones had to join forces. This led to the birth of the MLS, which was set up so that all brokers could put all their listings in one central location for all buyers to see. This ensured that brokers could work with the buyers who came to them and receive the appropriate commission even if they couldn't sell their own listings to the buyers. It was a win for brokers because they stopped losing clients, and a win for clients because they could see more inventory.

When brokers became too busy to handle all their clients, they hired agents to help service them and split the commission. Most brokers started off on 50/50 splits. The broker would create the lead then hand that lead off to the agent to serve. Agents closed deals and brokers made a profit. Brokers would take some of the money agents made for them and reinvest it in marketing and advertising. That's why you would see broker-specific commercials on television or ads in magazines.

This began to change when brokers like Keller Williams began teaching agents how to develop their own business and generate their own leads. In essence, they were teaching agents how to operate like brokers. Keller Williams went on to teach agents how to hire, train, and manage teams (also like brokers). More brokerages followed suit, and more agents began learning to build their own teams. This is now standard operating practice for many in the industry.

In today's environment, the broker plays a much smaller role. It's the agents who generate leads and run their business, with brokers doing very little to provide quality leads or opportunities. In most cases, brokers have been relegated to providing support resources and legal oversight. Brokers still want you to believe it's all about them, but nowadays it's not.

# Things Brokers Will Tell You That Don't Matter

## We Have a Strong Brand in the Community

Brokers often say this to boost their own ego and appear they are offering something they are not. The vast majority of home buyers and sellers have no idea which brokerage sells the most homes, has the most agents, or closes the most volume, and they don't care. Those are numbers brokers throw around simply to compete with each other.

What do buyers and sellers care about? They care about the feeling they get when they speak to the person who will be representing them, communicating with them, and advising them. That person is you. It doesn't matter which broker you choose when it comes to landing clients. It doesn't matter which broker sells the most houses and where. Don't fall for lines like this one.

## We Are the Cheapest Option

While I suppose this can be some form of value proposition, it's not a great one. Bragging about being the cheapest is like saying you are the Walmart of your industry. While Walmart-style value propositions do have their place in the world, representing people for the biggest financial transaction of their life isn't it.

You want to work with the broker you feel is the best, not the cheapest. Cheap commission splits mean less support, less guidance, and less opportunity for growth. I am very leery when someone's only advantage is how cheap they are. You usually get what you pay for. The only agents who should consider these types of brokers are those with experience who are looking to save money and don't need supervision or help.

## We Can Build Your Brand

Brokers should assist in building your brand, but they absolutely cannot do it for you. As a new agent, you want to focus more on training and less on branding. The more you know, the more confident you will be when you talk to people, and *nothing* will build your brand more than confidence. You want a broker who can show you a calendar of training they provide to their agents. Having a productivity coach to teach and train new agents is helpful too.

### We Have Technology Nobody Else Does

This is a legitimate benefit—when it's true. In my experience, it rarely is. Every brokerage tells you they have unique technology as a sales ploy to get you to sign up. New agents don't know what works, what doesn't, and what clients care about.

Take it from me: Most of your clients will never use the technology your broker provides unless it is *really* good. The majority will look at listings they like, choose the best ones, and ask you to arrange a showing. You will show them the listing and they will decide whether they want to write an offer or not.

While there may be little room for technology in the process of buying a home now, this will probably change in the near future. Be sure when choosing your broker to determine how much value they place on developing technology and integrating it into their business—but don't fall for the "we have the technology" bit.

## Things That Matter in a Brokerage

### Training

As a new agent, the first thing you should be looking for is training. This is the hardest thing to find but also the most important. Simply put, when you first get started, you don't know anything. It's very hard to find a mentor who will be willing to take the time to teach you. If you do find a mentor, I would highly encourage you join their brokerage.

Most good brokerages will offer training classes, courses, or online videos. Be sure to take advantage of these free educational courses but, of course, simply taking these classes won't help your sales performance—you'll have to put it all into practice! You should also join support groups with other new and experienced agents, sign up for a Premium membership on BiggerPockets.com, listen to podcasts, and search for training videos online. You can get great ideas from these resources, and they take some of the pressure off the broker to provide 100 percent of your training.

### Support

Support means providing people to help answer your questions when it comes to writing offers, filling out forms, navigating the MLS, and dealing with various scenarios new agents will encounter. When choosing a brokerage, ask who, specifically, will be providing this support and exactly what kind of support they will provide. Many brokerages say they will help you with email, a website, and business cards, but they won't offer any assistance when it comes to getting your first client into contract or negotiating a request for repairs. New agents should prioritize practical support over fancy marketing bells and whistles.

## Culture

The attitudes, mindset, and values of those who work at a brokerage determine its culture. As a new agent, if you join a brokerage with a fend-for-yourself mentality you will likely hate your job. The same goes for brokerages that operate like high-powered boiler rooms. Being a new agent is intimidating enough without these additional stressors.

If you enjoy socializing with coworkers, look for brokerages with friendly agents who see their colleagues as more of a family. At a company that encourages team outings or activities you can develop relationships with other agents more quickly, which will help you progress in your career. Conversely, if you're a "strictly business" type, you may hate this kind of environment. Ask questions and spend some time walking around the brokerage to see how everyone behaves, getting a feel for the specific culture you're signing up for.

## Growth Opportunities

Many brokerages offer opportunities for agents who excel to become employees. These positions can include sales manager, human resources coordinator, administrative assistant, or even branch manager. If you love real estate but skew toward the corporate side of things, you may want to ask about opportunities to supplement your income and work your way into other aspects of the business. Many agents develop leadership abilities in these roles that later help them thrive in their own businesses.

# Talking to Clients as a New Agent

As a new agent, you will find talking to clients intimidating. We all know what it's like to have that "please don't ask me how many houses I've sold" fear running through our heads. Most new agents have *nervousness* written all over them. This makes the client feel compelled to ask that dreaded question and reinforces the agent's anxiety.

Avoid having the question come up by getting the idea that you can't work with the client because you are new out of your head. Everyone is new at some point. If the question does come up, simply tell your client that the good news is they will get 100 percent of your time and attention. Clients will love that, and many of them will love the opportunity to help kickstart your career.

In order to avoid being asked questions you don't know the answer to, take control of the conversation. Don't wait for clients to ask you questions that leave you feeling compelled to reply right away or admit you don't know the answer. Instead, control the conversation by doing the asking yourself. Here are some things you can say:

- "I'd like to ask you a few questions for my research. Do you mind if I do that now?"
- "That's a very good question. Are there any more you can think of that I can write down and get back to you about later today?"
- "It's important for me to know what matters most to you. Other than what you just asked, can you tell me what else you'll need to know about?"

Phrasing questions this way helps set the expectation they won't be getting answers right away, and gives you the freedom to look up the answers without feeling pressured to answer on the spot. You can then consult with the person in your office responsible for supporting you and get accurate information to convey to your client without looking new or inexperienced. As a new agent, learning to control conversations is crucial.

## Talking to Other Agents

Perhaps the most intimidating part of being a new agent is having to talk to other, experienced agents to get additional information about a listing. I've watched new agents tremble at the mere thought of having to do this. I suspect they think everyone else knows the "right" way to approach other agents, but nobody has shown them what that right way is yet.

Most real estate agents do not sell a large number of homes. This is especially true in higher-priced markets, where a large percentage of agents are part-time and don't have to work as often. In fact, many of the agents you'll end up talking to won't be much more experienced than you. Some may even have many of the same questions you do, as well as the insecurities that go along with them. Understanding this is one of the best things you can do to boost your confidence before speaking to them.

In fact, there is no one "right" way to go about it. Trust your intuition because most of the questions that pop into your head are logical ones to be asking. To help you out, I've provided a list of frequently asked questions.

| FOR LISTING AGENTS | FOR BUYER'S AGENTS |
| --- | --- |
| Can you share how many offers you've received so far? | Can you share some feedback your clients gave you about the house after they saw it? |
| Where do you think the price will end up? | Can you share your opinion on how my listing compared with other properties you've shown? |
| Can you share how many disclosures you've issued so far? | Was there anything that concerned your buyers enough to prevent them from writing an offer? |
| What's the feedback been like from the buyer's agents? | How's the market been from your end? It seems like it's been (hot or cold) from my end. |
| How many showings are you getting a week? | Was there anything about the property you would recommend we change? |
| Are there any selling points about this property you can give me to share with my clients? | If we wrote your clients a reverse offer at (certain amount under list price), would they accept it? |
| If we wrote you a great offer before the deadline, would you take it? | Thank you for your offer. At this time, we have several other offers that are higher. Would you like to write at a higher amount, or are your clients already at their highest and best? |

Starting off every conversation by complimenting the other real estate agent is a great idea. They can be insecure about their business and volume (just like you), and a compliment can go a long way. I recommend the following opening lines:

- "I'm looking at your listing right now, and these pictures are gorgeous! You did a great job marketing this home. Can I ask you a few questions about it?"

- "I have a coming-soon listing in the area of your listing on 123 Main Street. Your property looks amazing and I see you sold it quickly, so I was hoping to get a little advice from you since you seem to be a top-notch agent. Can you tell me what your experience was like, and what you think I should do differently myself?"

## How to Dress

There's a ton of websites out there with the same basic information on how to dress professionally as a real estate agent, so I'm not going to restate the obvious. Instead, I'd like to give you some advice about how the way you dress can help or hurt you, as well as how to choose a style that complements your unique personality.

In general, if you have to choose between over- or underdressing, you should always err on the side of overdressing. When you dress better than your client expected, you convey respect and trustworthiness. It's a way of communicating that you take them, their concerns, and their money seriously without having to say a word.

When you dress professionally, people are more likely to treat you professionally. Can you sell a house in shorts and flip-flops? Of course. Dressing professionally won't sell the home, but it *will* get the attention of the person you're speaking to and make it easier for them to hear what you have to say. For an agent trying to help scared, uninformed, and nervous clients, this is vital.

When it comes to just how formally to dress, there is some wiggle room. At a minimum you should wear a collared dress shirt and slacks or a business-professional dress to a listing appointment, an appointment where you will be meeting a client for the first time, or an open house. It is perfectly acceptable to dress more formally than this as well. I wear suits to open houses and listing appointments and opt for business casual (e.g., dress shirt, slacks, a blazer and dress, and dress shoes or heels) when meeting clients in my office.

As you show homes, you'll still want to dress professionally but it's okay to take it down a notch. Because you'll be doing a lot of walking, standing, going up and down stairs, and getting in and out of your car, comfort is key. You also may be walking around outdoors, especially in yards—in all kinds of weather—and you don't want to get your clothing wet or dirty. I recommend agents always keep a change of nice clothes in the trunk of their car because you never know what the weather will throw at you—or when an opportunity to show a home or meet a potential client will arise.

## Common Real Estate Terminology

A quick and easy way to avoid new agent intimidation is to learn real estate industry terminology. The following cheat sheet covers most of the basics:

| TERM | DEFINITION |
|------|------------|
| Write or write on | To submit an offer or purchase agreement |
| Multiples | Multiple offers on the same property |
| Highest and best | The highest and strongest offer a client is willing to write |
| Seller multiple | A counter offer issued by a seller when they have received more than one offer from buyers |
| Buyer rep | A buyer representation agreement, also known as a buyer-broker agreement: a form that spells out the established exclusive relationship between an agent and a client |
| Listing agent | The agent representing the seller |
| Buyer's agent | The agent representing the buyer |
| Preapproval | A form issued by a lender indicating the price they are comfortable letting the client borrow money for, typically based on two years of tax returns and W-2s, two months of pay stubs and bank statements, and a credit check |
| Prequalification | A letter signifying the potential buyer has verbally stated their credit and financial information to the lender, but much of the information has not been verified |
| DTI | Debt-to-income, which is a ratio used by lenders to help determine how much a client can borrow |
| LTV | Loan-to-value, which is a ratio used by lenders to determine what percentage of a property's value is covered by the loan amount |

| TERM | DEFINITION |
|------|------------|
| Rate lock | The period of time for which an interest rate is locked on a loan and cannot rise |
| Rate lock extension | An option a borrower has to pay more money to extend the period of time a rate can stay locked |
| Extension | A request from a buyer to the seller for more time to comply with a contractual agreement (such as an inspection period extension) |
| Seller finance | When the buyer agrees to pay the seller a specified amount of money as a loan, as opposed to cash up front |
| Float the difference | When the seller agrees to accept the difference between an offer and the contractually agreed upon price as a seller-financed loan by the buyer |
| RESPA | Real Estate Settlement and Procedures Act: legislation that governs the various relationships in a real estate transaction |
| Addendum | A form used to spell out information agreed upon by both parties that was not included in the original offer |
| Counter | A response to an offer (or a counter offer) from the opposite party in a transaction |
| IDX | Internet Data Exchange: a website that has access to and acts as a portal to the MLS |
| Preemptive offer | An offer written before a deadline specified by the seller |
| Price point | The price range within which a buyer is looking to purchase, usually based on their preapproval letter |
| In escrow | Describes a house that is no longer actively for sale and is in contract with a buyer; also refers to the "escrow period" (the period in which an escrow is opened, deposits are made by the buyer, and due diligence is conducted) |
| Pending | A property that is in escrow and no longer actively for sale |
| Active | A property that is not currently in contract and is advertised on the MLS for sale |

| TERM | DEFINITION |
|------|------------|
| Sale price | The price a property sold for |
| List price | The price a property is listed for |
| Contingency | An agreement between parties in a contract that allows a buyer (or sometimes a seller) to back out of the deal and recover their deposit |
| Listing appointment | An appointment where an agent pitches their services and attempts to secure the listing by getting a signed listing agreement |
| Disclosures | State-specific paperwork that requires sellers to disclose known defects of the property |
| Pre-escrow | When the seller "opens escrow" with a title company before going into contract; intended to encourage the buyer to use the seller's title company |
| NHD | Natural hazard disclosure report |
| Inspection report | Report issued by licensed professionals speaking to the condition of the home |
| Section one | The section of a pest inspection report that describes evidence of the presence of a pest (such as rodent droppings or termite tubes) |
| Section two | The section of a pest report that describes items likely to lead to a pest infestation (such as an opening for mice to run into) |
| Termite report | A common phrase for a pest inspection report, even if it pertains to more than just termites |
| CMA | Comparative market analysis: a report showing a list of comparable active, pending, and sold properties |
| Short sale | A home being sold for less than the amount owed to the lender |
| REO | Real estate owned: a property a bank has foreclosed on and now holds title to |
| Lien | A debt owed from one party to another that is secured by an interest in the subject property; they are paid when ownership of a property transfers from one party to another |

| TERM | DEFINITION |
|------|------------|
| 1031 exchange | A swap of one investment property for another that allows the seller to defer paying capital gains tax; named for the relevant section of the IRS Code |
| Appraisal | A report issued by a licensed appraiser testifying to their opinion of a property's value |
| Due date | When selling a home, this is the date the seller has requested to review all offers with their agent |
| Title insurance | Insurance paid for by the buyer of a property to guarantee there are no missed liens or other issues with the condition of the property's title at transfer |
| Notice to perform | A form issued by one party in a transaction to inform the other party to take the requested action |
| Recording | When the title company notified the county assessor's office that title is being transferred from one party to another; and that is noted in the county's chain of title |

# Where to Find Answers to Commonly Asked Questions

When you are just starting out, your major challenge will be finding people who can competently and quickly answer your questions. This is especially tricky because you usually won't know what to ask until you need the answer. Therefore, it's wise to establish good relationships from the get-go with people who will be willing to answer your questions in a timely fashion. This way, you won't leave clients hanging.

This means you have to spend time in the office! Ask your new broker who the top-producing agents are and who is busy. My favorite strategy whenever I start a new job is to find out who the most successful and well-respected people are and get them to like me. I do this by offering to help them with things they dislike doing or by bailing them out of whatever jam they fall into.

For example, you could offer to do administrative work for busy agents. Preparing open house marketing materials, putting out open house signs, and looking up properties in the MLS are great ways to make yourself valuable to someone without a lot of spare time. If you play your cards right, making yourself useful is also a great way to find a mentor who can start teaching you the tricks of the trade. An experienced agent may do this for you if you make it worth their while. This is also a great way to learn how to show houses. Once you demonstrate that you're professional and competent, a busy buyer's agent might let you help show homes for their clients.

## The Benefits and Drawbacks of Being a Part-Time Agent

Some real estate professionals believe it's just fine to work as a part-time agent, while others insist that such agents are disrespecting the profession. I tend to see the issue not as being part-*time* but part-*dedicated*. If an agent is not 100 percent dedicated to their job, their profession, and their clients, they have no business being in the industry.

I myself started part-time. I worked my law-enforcement job four days a week and showed homes, held open houses, and attended listing appointments on the other three days. When I needed to complete real estate-related tasks on days I was working as a police officer, I would go to the office before work and get as much done as possible. When clients needed to talk during my shift, I would text to set up a time to talk to them later. Even though I had two part-time jobs, I was able to work both with full-time commitment because I did not have a family or other obligations. Your clients are placing a huge amount of trust in you, and they deserve your full commitment. If you plan to transition to a real estate career while hanging on to your current job, you should be aware of the benefits and drawbacks of this arrangement.

## THE BENEFITS

### Make Money While Learning a New Industry

The length of time it takes to earn money in this profession can be a problem for new agents. Many will work at least six months before seeing their first paycheck. If you hold on to your current job while learning this new one, you can avoid financial hardship before selling your first house. But be aware that while this will take the pressure off your finances, it will transfer that pressure to the rest of your life. Just because you aren't selling houses doesn't mean you won't be working! You won't have much time for a social life or much energy to devote to your loved ones.

If you choose this path, be sure not to shortchange yourself and give less than full effort to your new career. This can easily drag out from a six-month double-duty experiment to an eighteen-month nightmare if you're not totally committed. You can't learn real estate by just showing up at the office—you have to do the work. If you go through the motions on autopilot, you'll never make the leap to becoming a full-time agent.

### No Pressure from Commissions

Unfortunately, many agents will give bad advice to their clients (sometimes intentionally, sometimes not) in order to secure a commission. This happens most frequently when agents are under financial strain and need to earn money. Working a separate job while you learn the ropes of real estate sales will help you avoid this situation.

### Turn Coworkers into Clients

Of all the possible benefits, this is my favorite. So many new agents go to their real estate office to work, not realizing they'll never meet a client there. You're not going to find a client in an office full of real estate agents! As a salesperson you should be out and about meeting people, prospecting, and spreading the word about real estate. Why not do this at your day job while also getting paid?

I built my own clientele by talking about real estate to the guys I worked with on the police force. If you got stuck in a car or working a beat with me, you would hear about how real estate builds wealth. After a year of this, everyone knew I was the go-to person for real estate sales. My first clients were all cops. I built momentum this way and was able to get to the point where I was consistently closing two deals a month before going full-time.

This strategy is especially effective if your coworkers earn a good income and can afford to buy a home or, better yet, already own one. Work hard to make sure you have a great reputation and talk about real estate as much as people are willing to listen. If you can become the go-to real estate person in your company, you can find clients while also earning a paycheck.

# THE DRAWBACKS

### A Tighter Schedule

If you have to be at your full-time job all day, you obviously can't be showing houses or meeting with clients at the same time. This means you'll have to manage your schedule very carefully. When reaching out to clients, be sure to tell them up front when they can expect to hear from you. If you wait for them to call you first, you will always find yourself apologizing for being too busy or falling behind.

## Your Commitment Might Be Questioned

Because we are a fiduciary to our clients, the perception that we are not committed to their goals is a terrible shortcoming. If you have another job, you must make it absolutely clear to your clients that you want what they want just as much as they do. If you are not explicit about this, your clients can easily begin to see themselves as a side project to you. This is dangerous because to someone trying to buy or sell a home, little else in their life is as important.

## Less Likely to Make the Full-Time Leap

Perhaps you've heard the popular story about a military leader who led his troops into enemy territory, then ordered them to burn their boats behind them. This sent the message to the troops that surrender was not an option, and they were forced to move forward. There's wisdom in this approach. When turning back is not an option, people can feel extra motivated and get the most out of themselves.

In my experience, certain personalities need this type of inducement, but many others don't. It's never a bad idea to remove option B, at least from a motivational standpoint. When you work a second job and don't commit fully to real estate sales, it's easy for your subconscious to make excuses for why you shouldn't push out of your comfort zone.

Real estate sales offers massive earnings opportunities for one specific reason—very few agents are willing to push beyond their comfort zone. If they don't need the money or have some other compelling motivation, they can come up with a million excuses for why they are where they are, and, more importantly, why they aren't where they want to be. Take full advantage of the great opportunities that await you with real estate by jumping in with both feet.

# ⬛➡ KEY CHAPTER POINTS

- As a new agent, it's normal to feel intimidated. This feeling does not go away with time—it goes away with experience.
- Which broker you choose has a relatively small impact on your overall success.
- It doesn't matter whether a broker has a strong brand in the community.
- Working for a cheaper broker is not always the best option.
- Brokers cannot build your brand for you.
- The technology that a broker provides will not automatically make you successful.
- Ensure that your brokerage has a solid training program with support groups.
- Choose a brokerage that is consistent with your attitudes, mindset, and values.
- When talking to clients as a new agent, ask questions that will provide you more time to find answers for them.
- Dress professionally in order to be heard and trusted by your clients.
- Familiarize yourself with common real estate terminology.
- As a part-time agent, you can make money while learning a new industry and find new clients at your place of employment.
- The drawbacks to being a part-time agent include your lack of availability, the chance that you'll be viewed as insufficiently committed, and the lower probability that you'll make the leap to full-time.

## CHAPTER THREE

# YOUR FIRST THIRTY DAYS

Your first thirty days as a real estate agent are critical. While you're unlikely to sell a home during this time, you *will* be setting the habits that are going to serve you for the rest of your career. From the moment you first set foot in the office, it's crucial to have a plan in place to get off to a positive start.

A lot of what you'll be doing in your first thirty days involves setting up the infrastructure and systems you'll need to handle leads when they start coming in. While doing this, you must also make it a priority to get into the habit of daily lead generation. Throughout your career there will be ebbs and flows as the leads come in. You can't control how many people contact you, but you can definitely control the amount of effort you put into asking them to.

In fact, I always suggest agents start a Premium profile on Bigger-Pockets.com in their first thirty days in order to self-educate, generate easy leads, and connect with as many investors and agents as possible. The Premium membership allows you to private message members to make connections, join an exclusive forum with investors actively looking to grow their portfolios, and build a company profile—signaling to everyone on the site that you're an agent ready and willing to represent clients. Check it out at BiggerPockets.com/Premium and get started as soon as you can—you'll immediately find value as a new agent.

## Time Blocking

When you have a boss managing you daily, it's not always as important to build a schedule to monitor your progress since someone else is doing that for you. In the world of real estate, you are your own boss, so you must create a schedule for yourself—and then hold yourself accountable. In your first thirty days, you must learn how to set a schedule and stick to it. If you want to stay on schedule and remain productive, you'll need to block time off in your calendar for certain important tasks that have to get done.

Lead generation is the most important thing you'll do each day, so you should time block it first. Start your day with phone calls, text messages, and emails to those who know you, like you, and trust you the most. These are the people most likely to send you business. Maintaining these relationships is the most important thing you can do to ensure a steady stream of clients.

After lead generation, block off time for training, study, answering emails, looking up properties on the MLS, and so on. It's also a good idea to block off time to exercise, meditate or pray, eat, and watch training videos or listen to podcasts. When you have appointments to attend, post them in your calendar so you can time block around them. Look for ways to make phone calls while driving between appointments so you can be even more efficient.

## Software

As a real estate agent, you will be using several different software applications. This can be slightly overwhelming for new agents, especially if you aren't accustomed to using technology. One of the first things you'll want to do is write down all your login information—or subscribe to a password manager to keep all your logins in one place.

You'll probably use different software and need different logins for:
- Navigating the MLS
- Uploading executed documents for your brokerage to review
- Managing your database
- Finding the state-specific forms for writing offers and contracts

- Tracking leads in spreadsheets you'll create
- You'll also be using:
- Your office's specific CRM or database manager
- Your new real estate agent email
- Any training portals your office provides

Mastering new technology can be slow and awkward at first, but the quicker you can get the hang of it, the better you'll be at finding what you need and providing clients what they want. This will increase your productivity and your confidence, which will help you find even more clients down the road.

I recommend using a screencasting and recording tool called Loom to document how you use each application. With Loom you can record a video of your computer's screen and audio of your voice explaining step by step how to navigate each site or program. This will speed up your own learning process and provide a better alternative to taking notes. You can also use your videos as training tools for future team members or partners, helping them to learn more efficiently also.

## Database Creation

In your first week you'll want to get started creating a database of people you will use to generate leads. Until you begin telling people about your new profession and looking for clients, you haven't officially started work! I've come up with a system that allows you to do this quickly and efficiently, and gets you into the sales component of your business in a matter of minutes.

The first thing you'll want to do is take all the contacts in your phone and export them into a format that lets you quickly decide whether you want them in your database as a potential prospect. I recommend using a free app called MCBackup, but there are many similar apps available. What's important is to find one you are comfortable using and get started right away.

Assuming you're using MCBackup, follow these steps:
1. Download and open the app
2. Allow access to your contacts list
3. MCBackup will show you the total number of contacts in your phone

4. Hit "Export"
5. Hit "Email" after the contacts are exported
6. Ensure the file type is "CSV (Excel)"
7. Once completed, send the email to your email address
8. Open the email using an app like Excel, Numbers, or Google Sheets

Once you open this file, you'll notice it is in a spreadsheet format with headings like your database's names, phone numbers, and emails. Welcome to the start of your database! Now all you have to do is take out all the people you don't want in your database by deleting their information. Once that's done, notice which contacts are missing information such as their email or mailing address. Your job is to find ways to connect with these people in the next thirty days and start natural conversations, then ask them for their email once it feels organic. You can do this by offering to send them blog posts, articles, or videos you think they will find interesting and getting their email in order to send these.

Once you have completed this file, you can upload it to whatever customer relationship manager (CRM) software your broker provides. Or, if you find a CRM you like better, you can pay for it yourself and upload the information there. The CRM is what you'll use to keep track of your database's information. Many CRMs have features that make it easier to contact the people in your database and store information about your last phone calls with them. You're now set up to call the people in your database and tell them about your new profession as a Realtor!

## Social Media

Before I was a real estate agent, I never had a social media account. My original plan when I got my license was to keep it that way. It wasn't until I talked to other, more experienced agents that I realized this was a terrible idea. Social media is an incredibly powerful tool to stay top of mind with the people who know you without intruding into their life via phone calls or house visits. Consider the following stats from Hootsuite[1]:

- 90 percent of internet users say they watch video online at least once a month.
- 99 percent of users in 2019 accessed social media on mobile.

---

[1] Paige Cooper, "140+ Social Media Statistics That Matter to Marketers in 2020," February 20, 2020, accessed at https://blog.hootsuite.com/social-media-statistics-for-social-media-managers/.

- 43 percent of internet users use social media for work purposes.
- 43 percent of internet users use social media when researching things to buy.
- 63 percent of people say messaging apps are where they feel most comfortable sharing and talking about content.
- 92 percent of all Instagram users say they've followed a brand, clicked on their website, or made a purchase after seeing a product/service on Instagram.
- 1.95 billion of those users can be reached by ads. (That's 32 percent of everyone in the world over the age of 13.)
- 69 percent of US adults use Facebook.
- Last year people spent an average of two hours and twenty-four minutes on social media every day.

We can't get around the fact that social media is where the majority of Americans are spending a good amount of their time. As an agent, your goal is to be top of mind, so you need to get in front of those people where they are; and do it with interesting content that makes them want to see what you're up to—and want to reach out to talk to you about it. If you have hesitations about opening a social media account, I would highly encourage you to get over them!

In your second week of work, you should make sure you have opened Facebook, LinkedIn, and Instagram accounts. You can also consider starting a YouTube channel, downloading WhatsApp, and creating a Twitter account. Once you have a profile on these platforms, most of them will make it easier to add followers by recommending people you are likely to know based on the personal and demographic information you entered when you created your profile. Add all your old friends, colleagues, and coworkers. As you add more people, the social media apps will recommend more people for you to add. This is how you will build up your social media sphere.

When it comes to the content you post, do not jump right in and start talking about real estate out of the blue. I made this mistake when I first got my license, and I'm still paying for it. Nobody likes to feel they are just another faceless customer to you as you ask for referrals. Instead, focus on personal content, entertaining stories, or information likely to make your followers smile or chuckle. Get people used to seeing you in their feed before you start sharing real estate-related posts.

By your second month in the industry, if you've been posting consistently, you can start showing videos of homes you're touring and pictures of the best parts of the property. This will elicit interest in your audience and hopefully get them to reach out to you and ask about your new career or even the properties themselves. Even if they don't reach out, you can rest assured that people will have noticed, and you'll have piqued their curiosity. This will make your phone calls much easier when you finally talk to them, since they'll have things to ask you about.

## Initial Lead Generation

As a new agent you're going to have to get comfortable with the fact that you're going to be calling people to talk to them about real estate. You can try to avoid this, but you'll just be avoiding your own success.

In Chapter Five, I will cover many of the lead-generation strategies and sources you can use to engage with potential prospects naturally and effectively. For now, your main goal is to get everyone you have not talked to much in the past feeling comfortable with hearing from you and talking to you. You want to warm them up before you turn on the full force of your lead-generation machine! Start this process by using the CSV spreadsheet you created earlier and working from that. If you've already uploaded this information to a CRM, you can get into the habit of contacting the people from your CRM and entering notes there to document your conversations.

Begin with your closest friends and family members. These people are the most likely to support you in your new endeavor and will be much more gracious in dealing with the awkward missteps you're bound to make as you learn. Once you've established contact with them, move on to friends you know slightly less and former coworkers. Continue systematically working backward until you are talking to everyone you've ever meet about real estate, homes, and the condition of the market!

## Scripts

Since you're likely to feel a little uncomfortable talking to people about real estate when you never have before, consider using the following scripts. They offer easy ways to start conversations with people you haven't been speaking with regularly.

1. "Hey there, Jane. I was walking through the grocery store the other day and saw _____ and it reminded me of that time we _____. I wanted to give you a call and see how you've been! What's been going on lately?"

2. "Hey there, John. I know it's been a while, but I didn't realize how long! I think we haven't spoken since _____. I see from your Facebook a lot has changed! Looks like your family has grown, and the kids are getting so big now. Tell me, how have you been?"

3. "Hey, Pete. I saw you pop up on my Facebook feed, and I had no idea how much time had passed! I wanted to make sure the contact info I had for you was still good. Glad to hear it is. What are you doing for work these days? How have things been?"

The point of a script is to help you articulate the concept you want to convey. In this case your goal is to develop a dialogue that will ultimately lead the person to ask, "What have *you* been up to?" That will open the door for you to reply, "I'm in real estate. I help people sell houses. So glad you asked! Do you know anyone who's thinking about buying or selling I could talk to?" This is the easiest, most natural way to bring up your new profession without sounding pushy, greedy, or self-interested.

## The Benefits of Showing Homes

To be a successful new salesperson, you must put buyers into contract. Before you can do that, you'll need to become highly skilled at showing homes. Gaining experience at showing homes is a smart use of time in your first thirty days. Developing proficiency in this skill well help you in the following ways.

### Learning how to Set Appointments

Part of working with buyers is setting appointments to show homes. While this isn't the most difficult thing to learn, there are many details you need to get right. These include finding the showing instructions in the MLS, locating the lockbox, setting an appointment with the agent or seller, and scheduling a time to show homes in an orderly fashion. If you practice by setting appointments to go view the homes yourself, you will build confidence and learn more quickly.

## Navigating the MLS

The MLS can be tricky for new agents who aren't used to how it's set up. Since every MLS is different, I can't give specific instructions for how to navigate your local MLS, but learning as much as possible about it in your first thirty days should be a priority. You'll want to learn how to read the property page (location, price, status, days on market or DOM, agent remarks, and confidential remarks), how to put a search together to send to a client (practice sending to yourself first), how to set your client up on a drip campaign, and how to set up a comparative market analysis (CMA).

## Acquainting You with Inventory and Price Points in Your Market

Great agents know their market and what homes are available at which price points. Knowing this helps you sound like an expert when talking to new leads. It also gives you confidence when speaking with clients, especially when first establishing a rapport and, later, when advising them about what price to offer on a home. Top-producing agents are market experts. You can start the process of becoming one in your first thirty days.

## Making Videos and Taking Pictures for Social Media

Touring homes early can work synergistically with your social media goals as a new agent. Finding nice houses to preview gives you plenty of content to post and generate interest in your new profession. I recommend shooting videos as you walk through the property and make comments pointing out the best features. You can also point out unique things buyers may not have thought to look for themselves. This will inspire confidence in your ability to guide clients through the home buying process and indicates experience, even though you are brand-new.

## Providing You with Lead-Generation Conversations

Don't take this for granted! Those initial conversations are important, but they can be brutal. If you don't have topics prepared ahead of time, they can get awkward fast for all but the most skilled conversationalists. Take mental notes when showing homes so you have items to discuss during lead generation. Impressive backyards, superior craftsmanship, and attention-grabbing kitchens all make for great topics of conversation.

If you take pictures when showing the homes, you can send these to the people who seem interested. If there's one thing most people can agree on when it comes to real estate, it's that they love looking at beautiful homes! Even those who are not in the market to buy will enjoy seeing and talking about your adventures in real estate. This is especially true if you can tell an interesting story and pictures to go along with it.

## Training

Obviously, you'll want to seek out as much training as possible in your first thirty days. Different brokers offer different training options, so you should ask them what resources they offer and how you can get started. Some brokerages have online training modules for viewing. Others have manuals that spell out company policy, while others offer classes you can sign up for. As a new agent, you'll want to sign up for every single class you can possibly take. Ask for a training calendar if your office provides one and see what is available.

It's also important to seek training beyond your office. YouTube videos, podcasts, the resources available with Premium membership on BiggerPockets.com, and books like this one can all prepare you for your new career. Good content to help new agents can be hard to come by, but it's out there if you look for it. Some of my favorite podcasts are:

- *Real Estate Rockstars*
- *GSD Mode* with Joshua Smith
- *Real Estate Uncensored* with Greg McDaniel and Matt Johnson (be advised that this one has adult language)
- *Think Like a CEO* with Gary Keller and Jay Papasan
- *The Team Building Podcast* with Jeff Cohn
- *The BiggerPockets Podcast* with Brandon Turner (and me), of course

Listening to podcasts like these, where successful real estate agents share their experiences on building their businesses, can be educational and inspiring. Every agent achieves success in different ways, and it can take time for you to find someone who resonates with you and has a style you can emulate. Some agents are direct and business-oriented, while others are more personal and relationship-oriented. Finding your own authentic voice and style will be critical to your success.

On an episode of *Real Estate Rockstars* a few years ago, I heard the story of a young couple in Northern California who were selling several homes in their first six months in the business. Host Pat Hiban asked them how they were doing it, and they shared a secret to their success. Because they did not have a large number of clients that early in their career, they instead poured their energy into giving great service to those clients they did have. One way they did this was by showing up on moving day and literally loading up the moving truck along with their clients.

I thought this was brilliant, and as a relatively young and healthy man, I knew this was something I too could do to add value. Carrying heavy couches and moving boxes was right up my alley! I created a system in which the client would order the moving truck and have it ready on moving day. I would show up with a crew of movers I hired myself and help load everything from the old house into the truck to take to the new house. Doing this lessened the strain of the worst part about getting a new home. Clients loved it.

While I helped with the move, I would have my assistant send pizza and soda for everyone. This gesture would often go further in cementing our relationship than the $10,000 I saved them in negotiations! Taking care of small details like this showed clients I really cared about them.

In the meantime, I also got to meet all the most important people in their lives—best friends, parents, grandparents, cousins, the whole crew! Everyone got to see me in there sweating, carrying heavy furniture, and ordering food for my clients. This turned out to be the best referral source I could ever hope for. Each of those family members became clients of mine. When it was time for one of them to buy or sell a house, I was the agent they called.

This single small tip from a podcast resulted in several deals for me, and one huge payday. During my first year as an agent, I had a call with a client in which I ran the numbers on her property for her. We found she had so much equity that she could sell her home and buy a bigger one in a better neighborhood—with a pool. We agreed to list the house and sold it. Then we bought another one. While moving her furniture, I met her family members, who all then used me to buy houses too.

Building on that one original client, I ended up closing the following deals:

- Original listing: $670,000
- New home for original client: $950,000
- Grandmother's home: $780,000
- Aunt and uncle's home: $965,000

- New home for grandmother, aunt, and uncle to live in together: $1,350,000
- Friend from work who helped them move: $650,000
- Coworker who heard about their sale: $450,000
- Second coworker who heard about sale: $575,000

This was a total of $6,390,000 in gross sales volume from *one* day of helping a client move. And I never would have thought to do that on my own. You may not be into moving heavy boxes, but you *will* find something that resonates with you on these podcasts. Make it a priority to listen to several a day in your first thirty days.

## Creating Strong Habits

The habits you establish in your first thirty days in the business will follow you for the rest of your career, so create good ones! You will never be more eager and impressionable than at this stage in your new professional life. This is the time to practice your time blocking, educate yourself, and get into the routine of daily lead generation. Top-producing agents have habits that support their goals. When they make a promise to themselves, they keep it. This means they are in the office when they said they would, and they call as many potential leads as they said they would.

Get this part right early in your career and you'll be glad you did. I recommend every new agent make a minimum of twenty voice-to-voice phone calls each day in which they mention they are in real estate and ask for business. This may sound challenging at first, which is why you must time block for it. If you find it difficult to stay on task, print out a list of the twenty people you will call the night before and place it on your desk. The next day, arrive at the office on time and start making those calls, going down the list one by one and making notes in your CSV file or CRM as you go.

While setting these habits may seem trivial at the start of your career, I assure you that they will have a *massive* impact on your success as an agent. Get started on the right foot and you'll never look back!

# ⬛➤ KEY CHAPTER POINTS

- Your first thirty days as a real estate agent are a critical time to build effective habits that will serve you for the rest of your career—sign up for a Premium account on BiggerPockets to get started quickly.
- Use time blocking during your first thirty days to make sure you accomplish the most important tasks, such as lead generation and training.
- Familiarize yourself with all the software applications you'll need to do your job, and use Loom to record screencasts with instructions for review at a later time.
- Export all the contacts in your phone with MCBackup or a similar app to start building your database.
- Create social media profiles and begin building relationships and posting content on a regular basis.
- Start lead generating with your friends and family first.
- Practice several "opening" scripts you can use to start conversations with friends.
- Tour homes on a regular basis to learn how to set appointments, navigate the MLS, understand the market and inventory, and create content for social media promotion.
- Educate yourself by taking advantage of any training provided by your broker, reading books, watching YouTube videos, signing up for a free membership on BiggerPockets.com, and listening to podcasts.

## CHAPTER FOUR

# INTRODUCTION TO THE SALES FUNNEL

Real estate agents are 100 percent responsible for their own success. Few other jobs can claim the same. You won't have a boss, a manager, or a supervisor telling you what to do. You won't have specific office hours dictated by someone else. You won't know when you're on the clock and when you're not. You won't ever be "at work," but you also won't ever be "off."

Most jobs have clear-cut lanes within which you must learn to operate. Much like the lanes in a swimming pool, there is one direction to go, and the only thing you have to worry about is the speed at which you do it. Being a real estate agent is more like being dropped in the middle of the ocean. You can swim any way you want, with no one to tell you what to do or where to go. You have complete freedom with very few rules or restrictions—and that is exactly why most agents will fail.

Complete freedom may sound enticing if you don't like your boss or feel restricted at your job. But most people do not thrive in an environment lacking direction or supervision. It's very easy to get lost in the ocean and just float around all day! As an agent, you are your own boss. You make your own schedule, set your own rules, and succeed or fail based on your own actions.

If you want to stay on the right path, you must have a very clear understanding of what that path is, when you have strayed from it, and how to progress along it. After having learned to navigate the big, scary, confusing ocean myself, I've come up with a system for staying on track and moving forward. I call it the sales funnel.

The sales funnel is designed to help you take every single piece of information that comes your way and understand where it fits into the big picture. It simplifies the incredibly vast ocean of information you'll be swimming in and provides you with structure. The sales funnel is how I create my own swimming lanes so I can make progress while my competition flounders.

## Everything Is a Funnel

Real estate sales, like any other business, is a funnel. I credit *The BiggerPockets Podcast* host and best-selling author Brandon Turner for pointing this out. You start with a large group of potential leads. Then, through a careful process of refining, effort, and qualification, you end up with a much smaller group of highly qualified candidates at the other end. The process of making your way from a large group of potential candidates to a much smaller group of more valuable candidates is what we refer to as the funnel process.

The best agents, as well as the best business owners in general, are good at two things:

1. Putting large numbers of people into the top of their funnel.
2. Moving those people from one stage of the funnel to the next.

For context, let's look at how this process works in other businesses and organizations. The following are examples of using funnels to earn profits and achieve results.

- An oil refinery takes a large amount of unprocessed fossil fuel and converts it into a smaller amount of useful gasoline.
- A sports team brings in a large number of players for tryouts, then systematically makes cuts until only the best are left.
- A company advertises job opportunities to a large number of candidates, then pushes them through an application process to weed out the least qualified.
- A real estate agent has a large database of people they've met, and systematically moves those people from a name to a lead to a client to a sale.

The goal of this book is to help you become more efficient at moving people along the funnel of your business. This is the first skill to develop on your path to becoming a top-producing real estate agent.

Before we dive into the details, let's begin with an overview of the process. Losing sight of the big picture leads to wasting time on activities that don't make you money. Keeping the sales funnel goals top of mind is the best way I've found to navigate my day with purpose and clarity. Learn the path—and the process—so you can stick to it and not get lost along the way.

## Sales Funnel Stages

The real estate sales funnel is broken down into five stages: people, leads, clients, contracts, and closings. In order to successfully move clients down the stages of the funnel, you must master the tools required to move them along to the next stage. When a client reaches the bottom, you get paid. If a client does not reach the bottom, you get nothing.

In a funnel format, the five stages look like this:

As complicated as real estate sales can seem, this graphic will help you remember how simple it should really be. This is how you convert a client into a paycheck.

## Stage One: People

At the top of our funnel, we will start with finding people whom we can turn into leads. (The process of converting people into leads is called "lead generation" and will be covered in depth in Chapter Five.) Because this is the first step in the funnel, you will find yourself spending most of your time on this stage, especially when you are new to the business.

One of the best parts of real estate sales is that people are literally everywhere. You can find them by just walking outside. Don't like to walk outside? Get on your phone and call someone. Don't feel like talking today? Send an email. Don't want to send an email to one person? Create an online marketing campaign. Too lazy to do that? Post on social media about your current interests and see who engages with you. People are everywhere. You just have to be creative with how you find and connect with them.

One of the key factors in getting people to engage with you (the first step toward winning them over to work with you) is the way you conduct yourself. Keep in mind some of the following statistics put out by the National Association of Realtors in 2019[2]:

- 41 percent of buyers used an agent who was referred to them by a friend, neighbor, or relative.
- 12 percent of buyers used an agent they had previously used to buy or sell a home.
- 39 percent of sellers used an agent who was referred to them by a friend, neighbor, or relative.
- 27 percent of sellers used an agent they had previously used to buy or sell a home.

People will constantly be evaluating you—not just when you meet them in person but also when they are researching you. Maintaining a professional, knowledgeable, and confidence-inspiring appearance at all times is crucial. There is no such thing as a "business profile" and a "personal profile." Your business brand is your personal brand. Being an agent is a full-time commitment that spans across all aspects of your life! Unprofessional posts, offensive political commentary, and rude or offensive language will turn off many potential clients. Keep this in

---

2  National Association of Realtors, "2019 Profile of Home Buyers and Sellers," November 2019, accessed at https://www.nar.realtor/sites/default/files/documents/2019-profile-of-home-buyers-and-sellers-highlights-11-07-2019.pdf.

mind: If you want to be successful convincing people to think of you when they need real estate services, you want to make it as easy as possible for them to choose you.

As you become more successful and progress in your career, you'll find yourself spending less time looking for new clients and more time servicing clients who have come to you from past efforts. When that happens, you'll begin the process of hiring others to help service your clients and move them along the funnel, giving you more time to get back into lead generation to increase your business even more.

## Stage Two: Leads

A lead is a person who knows who you are and wants to buy or sell a home. Top producers are continually targeting leads as the primary focus of their business. Gary Keller, cofounder of Keller Williams, has said, "If you are a salesperson, you have two jobs. One is your chosen vocation; the other is lead generation." Finding leads is the most important thing an agent can do.

Since people are higher on the funnel than leads, you may think finding people is the most important thing you can do. After all, that is the true top of the funnel. People, however, won't voluntarily move down your sales funnel unless they are motivated to buy or sell a house. Since motivation is essential to moving someone down the funnel, you are better off by starting to look for leads within the "people" category.

It's easy to make the mistake of investing time, energy, and emotion in people who aren't motivated to buy or sell. Having a great conversation with an unmotivated lead who takes hours of your time, really likes you, and asks for your knowledge, expertise, and insights can make you feel useful and good about yourself. The problem is if they aren't motivated, you won't be able to move them down the funnel. Don't make the mistake of working for emotional gratification at the expense of profit.

While it *is* important to spend your time sharing knowledge about the industry and talking to people about real estate, it is equally important to correctly classify the person you are speaking with. If you are talking to someone about real estate to let them know who you are and get them to call you when they want to buy or sell, that would be correctly classified as the "people" stage. Don't make the mistake of considering someone a lead just because they are interested in real estate. Remember that a lead is someone who knows who you are *and* wants to buy or sell a house.

Learning to quickly identify which of the people you speak with are truly motivated will ensure that you spend your time wisely, that is, moving people from the top of the funnel to the bottom and focusing on that as much as humanly possible throughout the day.

Here's a helpful tip I use in my own business. When I am speaking to people for the purpose of converting them to leads, I share all I can about real estate. I will tell them how I analyze properties, what techniques I use to get hot properties under contract, and how the market works. I'll share information about property taxes, homeowner's insurance, and how to avoid PMI (private mortgage insurance). I do all this to earn their trust and become their real estate agent of choice when they have something to buy or sell.

Once someone has called me or presented themselves as a lead, it's less important to spend time providing them with information and more important to get them in front of me so I can deliver a presentation on exactly what I can do to help them. In-person meetings are a crucial step in developing a strong rapport and an emotional connection with the lead. Appointments and presentations are the tools I use to move leads to the next step of the funnel and secure them as clients. I provide only as much time, information, and energy as necessary to secure an appointment. The appointment is where I really blow them away!

When I'm trying to get you into my funnel, my goal is to create interest and trust so I can get your contact information to put in my database (the top of the funnel). Once you're in my funnel, I focus on directing my energy toward activities that will move you along the funnel. This requires discipline. It does not always feel natural to be so purposeful.

Being purposeful is important because many people will be happy to take everything you give them—your precious time, energy, emotions, and even gas! It's not uncommon for them to then turn around and use another agent after you've invested so much in them. Protect your resources and stamina by remaining focused on looking for leads who will use you as their agent and moving those leads to the next step of your funnel. Funnel progression is a hallmark of a top-producing agent. If you are merely *hoping* the client will choose you, you will lose them to the agent who took purposeful action to move them to the next stage, making them a client.

## Stage Three: Clients

The client stage is what most new agents think of when they imagine a typical workday. At this stage you will be looking up properties on the MLS, writing offers, showing homes, and running CMAs. The client stage is the point at which you have earned the right to do the work of an agent (represent clients, help them make decisions, and make their dreams come true). It is also the stage at which clients have earned the right to your full attention.

A client is someone who has signed either an exclusive buyer representation agreement or an exclusive listing agreement with an agent. A "person" or a "lead" does not earn the right to command your full attention until they have signed the appropriate paperwork and become a client.

If you give everyone who crosses your path your full attention, you will quickly find yourself out of time to put toward revenue-generating activities. Many agents run their business much more loosely and offer their full services without expecting a commitment in return. This is not in line with sound business practices—have you ever been to the doctor for free?

If you act as if you are not worthy of the same respect as other professionals, you will be treated accordingly. What's worse, it will have a negative impact on your bottom line. Too many agents give away their expertise for free and then complain when a prospect doesn't use them. You'll hear this when you walk through your brokerage if you listen: constant mumbling and griping about disloyal clients, unfair treatment, and getting a raw deal. Don't take the bait and go down that rabbit hole yourself. Complaining does not move people down your sales funnel and is a waste of energy.

Instead, focus on giving leads just enough attention and information to make them *want* to work with you. Your goal is to set the appointment and deliver a stellar presentation that shows them exactly why you are their best option. Once they've committed to working with you, it is appropriate to match their level of commitment. Committing yourself to those who have committed to you is common sense and good business.

I am a real estate investor. As such, many people come to me looking for information on buying out-of-state homes, analyzing rental opportunities, or flipping homes. Giving away my knowledge and time to anyone who asks is a drain on my business. Instead, I give them enough information to show that I am a competent, skilled professional. Then I let them know I offer this knowledge freely to those who are my real estate clients and ask them to become one.

This simple script allows me to set appointments, draw in leads, create clients, and close deals. You may not be a real estate investor (or maybe you are and can do the same as I do), but you are still an expert in something the client needs. Maybe it's local trends, average days on market, or the best school districts. Use this to draw in leads to become clients. Then share this information freely with your clients when appropriate.

Clients are the lifeblood of your business. Creating them is the single most important thing you can do in order to earn money in the future. Much of a top producer's activity centers on creating appointments to deliver presentations and secure clients as soon and as frequently as possible. Save the best of your attention and effort for those who are as committed to you as you are to them.

## Stage Four: Contracts

Once the offer contract has been signed by both parties, an escrow company is notified, an escrow number is assigned, and the contractual obligations of both parties are put into effect. At this point, both parties are currently in "escrow." Putting clients into contract and opening escrows is an incredibly important part of running a profitable real estate business.

The escrow stage is the easiest one at which to leverage help from others. Successful agents tend to start with the stages nearest the bottom of the funnel and begin leveraging off that work first, then make their way back up the funnel. Administrative assistants, transaction coordinators, and similar professionals do most of their work at the escrow stage. They make up the first level of assistants you'll hire to free up your time for more income-generating activities.

Once you've successfully created a consistent stream of properties and clients in escrow, you can start hiring assistants to complete the tasks necessary to close them. This will give you more time to move one step higher on the funnel and create more success there. As you gain success at each successive level up, you can hire and train others to take over that stage as well.

A funnel is only effective if the person it's funneling consistently moves down. If there's a logjam at any stage in the funnel, you'll be forced to slow down the activities closer to the top that generate the most revenue (lead generation and setting appointments) in order to clear the jam at lower levels (putting people into contract and keeping deals alive in escrow). Gaining mastery at the lower levels of the funnel is required to leverage off the work. You'll need to be able to train others to do it.

The catch is in order to gain mastery, you'll need experience. The best way to get that is to put a lot of people into contract! As you successfully move people down the stages of the sales funnel, you'll gain more and more experience with dealing with problems in escrows. Many new agents make the mistake of trying to learn how to put out fires related to loans, title, or inspection reports before they learn how to find and convert clients. In fact, it may seem easier to focus on problem solving rather than getting good at lead generation. You can learn how to put out fires all you want, but you'll never be able to apply that knowledge if you don't have people moving down the funnel. For this reason, I always recommend new agents start off perfecting lead generation and crushing appointments and presentations before focusing on the more complex elements of a transaction.

Once you've secured a client as your own, the next step in the process is to get them into contract on a property. For buyers, this means getting a purchase agreement accepted. For sellers, this means obtaining an offer for your listing that your clients accept. Putting properties into contract on a consistent basis is the hallmark of a top-producing agent. Every step in the funnel up to this point exists solely to help you find clients to put into contract.

The best agents don't take listings they can't sell (that is the mark of a weak agent). If you do your job well, the majority of listings you take will sell. In most markets, it is easier and less time-consuming to find a buyer for your listing than to put a listing under contract for a buyer. That's why securing listings should be your No. 1 priority. For buyer clients, you'll be doing the following to assure them they are making a wise decision and submitting a prudent offer that will meet their goals:
- Running comparable sales or average rents in the area
- Looking up neighborhood reports
- Estimating commuting times or school scores
- Estimating rehab costs
- Ensuring the home meets the client's original criteria
- Running mortgage payment calculations

- Researching HOA fees and conditions
- Calling listing agents and feeling them out to see whether you can obtain the property at the price your client wants
- Communicating property details to the lender
- Reviewing inspection reports or seller disclosure packets
- Reviewing applicable covenants, conditions, and restrictions
- Talking to your client and easing their concerns
- Looking up property tax records and special assessments
- Helping to get estimates for home insurance
- Reviewing zoning restrictions

For seller clients, you'll be looking for buyers for their property as well as advising your clients on how to choose the offer that is best for them. This may involve the following activities:
- Writing a description of the property
- Arranging for the home to be photographed
- Entering your listing into the MLS
- Scheduling showing appointments
- Holding open houses or knocking on doors in the neighborhood to advertise your listing
- Making calls in the neighborhood to advertise your listing
- Ensuring the house and yard are kept tidy and clear
- Reviewing buyer feedback and online views
- Informing prospective buyer agents of relevant data
- Reviewing and negotiating offers received
- Calling lenders to verify preapprovals
- Following up with agents who have shown the property
- Keeping your client in the loop regarding recent activities and action

The *only* part of the real estate funnel process where you actually make money is when you put people into contract *and* they close on the home. Lead generation and setting up appointments are all about converting people into clients who are ready to write an offer on a property.

Steps four and five are all about saving the money you've already made. The most important revenue-generating activity for your business is putting houses under contract and getting the buyers to closing! If you could choose only one activity at which to excel, or one activity to do yourself while delegating everything else to others, it should be this.

If you can master step three, you'll be much more motivated to do a good job on steps one and two. You'll also be more motivated to hire administrative talent to help with steps four and five. Top-producing agents excel at step three. By the time you're done with this book, you will have all the tools to excel at it as well.

Leading your clients down the funnel and putting them into contract will bring your first sigh of relief. While this is the point at which your job as their agent actually begins, it is also the point at which clients are the most committed to the process and least likely to change their minds. Putting clients into contract is the most fun stage for me as an agent. It is also the most rewarding. Moving people from leads to clients to putting them into contract will build your confidence and your love of the profession and help you build the momentum that will eventually make the job easier.

During the escrow process, the buyers of the home are conducting their due diligence to make sure they want to complete the purchase. This due diligence is determined by the laws of the municipality and the terms of the offer. However, the escrow process always includes the following steps:

- Obtaining title insurance
- Submitting an earnest-money deposit
- Running title reports
- Obtaining full loan approval
- Obtaining an appraisal
- Completing home inspections, pest inspections, roof inspections, and other due diligence
- Verification of the neighborhood
- Buyer walkthroughs
- Further negotiations

In most states, contracts are written and submitted by buyers. This means the majority of the contract is intended to protect the buyer, and consequently the majority of the escrow process leaves the buyer in the driver's seat. Buyers typically have contingencies, or "outs" to a contract, while sellers do not. This allows a buyer to change their mind and back out of the deal. Sellers do not commonly have the same rights or abilities.

Understanding how to take advantage of a buyer's ability to back out of a deal puts the buyer's agent in a powerful position. Limiting the ability of a buyer to back out of a deal puts the listing agent in a stronger position.

Understanding what occurs during escrow is crucial to negotiating the offer in a way that will leave your client in a strong position. Knowing how to articulate these intricacies will leave you as the agent in a much better position to keep your client engaged, invested, and willing to see the deal through to the end.

The ability to manage the escrow process is twofold. First, an agent must understand the law, the contract, and their client's options. You must continually weigh the benefits versus the risks and advise your client on what they stand to gain versus what they stand to lose. Second, you must skillfully and calmly manage your client's emotions. Very few people make decisions from an entirely rational mindset, and your clients are no exception. By acting as a buffer to help absorb fear, uncertainty, anger, and frustration, you will enable your client to make wise decisions while experiencing emotional turmoil.

Many agents never master both sides of managing the escrow process. This shows up in several ways. In addition to having more houses fall out of contract, these agents usually succumb to frustration and negativity. This hurts their lead generation, lead follow-up, ability to put additional houses into escrow, and more.

If you want to have a growing, thriving business, *you* must be growing and thriving. Developing the necessary skills as well as a positive mindset is a crucial part of becoming a top-producing agent. To successfully complete step four you must act with authority and expertise to advise your client on the steps they should take, keeping them motivated to continue moving down the sales funnel.

## Stage Five: Closings

The fifth and final stage of the funnel is the closing. A closing is a successfully completed escrow in which the title changes hands and the agent is paid their commission.

It is extremely important to understand one simple thing: If a deal does not close, you do not get paid. Period. It does not matter how good a job you did or how grateful your clients are. You will not earn any money if you are not closing deals.

This may sound obvious. However, I point this out because it is far worse to move a person to the last stage of the funnel only to have the deal fall through than to have failed to convert the lead into a client in the first place. Bringing a deal all the way to escrow and then losing the closing will take more of your time, energy, effort, and money than losing a lead in stage two. The only exception is when an escrow doesn't close but the client is retained and put into contract a second time.

That's why it is so important to have signed exclusive buyer representation and listing agreements. There is no guarantee deals will close. In fact, many deals do not because of complications beyond the agent's control. Without a contract securing the client, you may find yourself doing a lot of work, spending a lot of time, and facing a lot of frustration—all to have the deal fall apart and the client move on to a new agent.

I first experienced similar situations as a waiter when 90 percent of my income came from tips. If things went wrong for reasons beyond my control—say, the steak was overcooked or the cocktail was too strong (or too weak)—the customer often took it out on me in the form of a poor tip. Even though I had no control over the cook's or bartender's performance, my income depended on it.

I learned a powerful fact: *Most people care more about results than they do about the specific performance of any individuals involved.* The customer who had to wait for a new steak while everyone else was eating expressed their displeasure by tipping me less, even though I had nothing to do with the mistake.

Likewise, if your real estate clients don't get the results they want, they won't be happy with you—even if you performed your job flawlessly. This can happen when:

- The buyer looks at multiple properties but cannot bring themselves to make a competitive offer.
- A buyer doesn't get the house at the price they wanted.
- The seller goes with another offer because the buyer took too long to make a decision.
- The seller receives multiple offers, doesn't counter your client, and chooses a better offer instead.
- A home inspection comes back worse than the buyer anticipated.
- A home appraises below the contract price.
- Interest rates increase during the escrow period.
- Title and escrow fees are higher than the buyer anticipated.
- The lender fails to respond to your clients in a timely manner.
- The lender fails to warn the buyer about closing costs.
- Underwriting takes too long to approve the loan.
- The seller leaves the home dirty or cluttered for the new owners.

- The seller insists on listing a property too high and buyers don't come to see it.
- A listing doesn't generate any solid offers.
- The feedback from those viewing your listing is unflattering.
- A home in the neighborhood with more upgrades sells for more.
- The title company fails to inform the seller about notary fees.

The key to a successful closing and a happy client is to manage expectations. If you can keep your clients happy, successfully close escrows, and meet their expectations, you can take those satisfied clients and turn them into referral partners. Making sure a high percentage of your clients are pleased with your performance is the absolute best way to ensure future business and growing sales numbers.

When you reach the closing stage, you want to make sure as many people as possible see that you were successful in helping your client reach their goals. You can do this by:
- Posting about the successful transaction on social media.
- Tagging your clients in a social media post so their followers see the good news.
- Telling your friends and family about it afterward, when you are excited and passionate.
- Asking for referrals from the client when you deliver the keys to their new home.
- Asking for referrals from your sellers when you call to congratulate them and tell them to expect the money to be transferred to their account.
- Telling everyone in your sphere of influence about the successful transaction when they ask what's new in your life.
- Arranging for a pizza party or some other gift to be delivered to your client's workplace for all their coworkers to see.
- Introducing yourself to the neighbors in the community and informing them that a house just sold, what the price was, and how many offers you received.
- Sending a closing gift to the buyers of your listing to congratulate them on their new purchase. (They may be unhappy with their current agent, especially if you out-negotiated them.)
- Sending "just sold" postcards or mailers throughout the neighborhood to introduce yourself and share your contact information.

By sharing the news of your success, you increase the number of people who hear your name and see your prowess. By meeting these people and adding them to your database, you create the opportunity to form a relationship with them and convert them into leads when the time comes. This creates a new person to start down the sales funnel, fully completing the cycle! Doing this repeatedly is what top producers focus on. It is the bedrock of a successful business and the most cost-effective way to grow your numbers, experience, and success.

The final step of the sales funnel is also the sweetest one—closing! As a fully commissioned sales agent, you receive money only when your clients close. Failing to close means failing to run a healthy business. For top-producing agents, that is unacceptable. It's true that not every deal will close. It's also true that the vast majority of them should.

Some may feel it's dishonest or greedy to believe deals should go all the way to closing. I disagree. When a deal fails to close, it's not just the agent who suffers. *Everyone* suffers. The buyers of the property spent money on inspections and appraisals they now have nothing to show for. They spent time and energy worrying about a property they didn't end up owning. Interest rates may have risen, and prices may have as well.

Sellers lose too. Sellers make their home available, put up with intrusions, and go to bed every night not knowing what is coming next or whether the deal will close. Sellers who begin the process of searching for their next home before the escrow process is completed will find those efforts wasted if the deal doesn't close. Furthermore, sellers have little say in whether a deal closes or not, since buyers sit firmly in the driver's seat. It feels very unfair to most sellers when a buyer fails to perform or backs out of a contract.

In addition to the clients, other businesspeople suffer too. Lenders put a lot of work, time, and effort into a deal. When it doesn't close, they don't get paid. This means they lose out on all the potential business they could have developed in steps one and two of their own funnels. Title and escrow companies lose out. They do all the work necessary to close the deal and ensure they are not the holdup—then end up not being paid for their time.

Top-producing agents look out for their clients, their coworkers, and those involved in the transaction who are vulnerable and unable to affect the outcome. They operate with a high degree of integrity and do their jobs to the best of their ability. If you want to be a top real estate agent, you need to bring deals to close. This shows your clients that you don't start a job you don't intend to finish. Once a deal closes, you should market your successful venture for future clients to see. Doing this well results in several benefits to your business, *none more important than making it easier for you to start your next sales funnel!*

# Funnel Tools

### Overview

The stages of the sales funnel help us classify where a prospect falls within the system. Once you correctly classify a prospect, you can then focus on what the next appropriate action will be. The classifications are road markers to remind you where you are on the journey and, more importantly, where you're going next.

The tools are the actions you must take to move people through the sales funnel. Developing these tools will be the main focus of your efforts to become a top producer. The sharper your tools, the less effort you'll need to put into using them, and the more effective you'll be!

You'll find the tools listed on the right side of the sales funnel.

Top-producing agents have mastered these tools and are able to move people from one stage to the next with ease, efficiency, and a high rate of conversion. If you are serious about improving your sales numbers and building a successful real estate business, you *must* focus on improving your effectiveness with these tools.

## Start with the Three F's

When new agents join my team, I make them practice these various tools on the Three F's:

- Friends
- Family
- Future clients

These three groups are where every agent should start their lead generation (first tool). These people are the most likely to be invested in building your business and seeing you succeed. They are also the most forgiving! It's much easier to make mistakes or have awkward conversations with those who already know and love you. Take advantage of these relationships to grow your skills, confidence, and comfort level.

These are also the best people to practice delivering presentations that you'll give during your appointments (second tool). You're always going to be nervous when explaining something for the first time. The nerves get even worse when it's something as important as walking someone through the process of buying or selling a home. The intensity grows when you sense fear in your clients because they don't know what to expect and are leaning on you to be their guide.

The path to confidence and comfort is repetition. You simply need to have lead-generating conversations and deliver your presentations with enough frequency that they become natural and easy. The Three F's will be your best friends when it comes to finding a safe and forgiving place to practice these tools.

This holds true for developing your mastery of human psychology (third tool) as well. As an agent dealing with anxious clients, you will learn much more about what makes human beings tick than you ever thought possible. In fact, I spend more time reading, studying, and pursuing knowledge about the human mind and emotions than I do about real estate itself. As you find yourself constantly challenged by new situations and different personalities, you will see that top-producing agents are counselors just as much as they are advisors. Forcing yourself to put these new skills into play with the Three F's is the easiest and safest way to find out what works and what doesn't.

Finally, you can also grow your real estate knowledge (fourth tool) through conversations with the Three F's. If you fail to anticipate a client's question or are forced to solve a problem mid-escrow, there's a strong chance you'll be caught off guard and have to admit your ignorance. While there's nothing wrong with an honest "let me look into that and get back to you," it's still not an ideal answer. Inexperienced agents can find themselves calling their broker at 10 p.m. to ask questions mid-crisis, and brokers aren't usually too fond of this.

It's always better to start curiosity-based conversations with your friends, family, and future clients. When you don't have all the answers, they won't judge you nearly as harshly. This also gives you the opportunity to recognize where the deficiencies in your knowledge are so you can start looking for answers before you need them. Some of the ways I encourage new agents to talk about real estate with their families and friends are to ask them:

- What intrigues you most about real estate?
- What are your biggest questions about real estate transactions?
- What scares you the most about buying a house?
- What is your favorite way to look for a home?
- Do you know the difference between a broker and an agent?
- What do you think is most important when choosing an agent?
- Do you know how much commission an agent keeps?
- Are you aware of what agents pay for licensing, MLS access, desk fees, etc.?
- Do you know how lenders are compensated?
- Do you understand what contingencies in a contract are and how they are used to protect the buyer's deposit?
- Do you understand how homes are valued/appraised?
- Do you know what to expect in closing costs, and what those closing costs are used for?
- Have you ever seen a home inspection report, and would you like to review one together?
- Do you understand what PMI is and how to avoid it?
- Do you know how property taxes are determined, and how to avoid the parts of town where they are highest?

The point of these conversations is to expose you ahead of time to questions you will have to answer at some point in your career. These conversations will reveal gaps in your knowledge and provide you with the opportunity to ask your broker for answers (or look them up in this book or at another resource, like BiggerPockets.com) when it's not 10 p.m.! You'll also find that the more you know, the more confidence you have, and the more confidence you have, the more likely you'll be to talk about real estate. This will absolutely lead to more business opportunities as you'll stay top of mind with more people.

Top producers talk about real estate constantly. They own the mind-share in their sphere of influence when it comes to real estate—and that is a valuable space to own! If you aren't confident in your own knowledge, you won't feel inclined to put yourself in a position where that will be exposed. This will negatively impact your business and prevent you from reaching your potential.

Start with the Three F's and practice the tools on them first. Improving your proficiency with them is the single best thing you can do to increase the number of deals you close and the amount of money you make.

## Tool One: Lead Generation

The very first tool in the sales funnel is lead generation, which is what we use to convert people into leads. Because leads are the most important asset you can develop in your business, lead generation is the most important tool for you to learn, master, and use on a daily basis.

The best agents create time in their calendar for lead generation and build everything else in their business around that cornerstone. This means they do not let anything infringe upon that time in their schedule. That includes:

- Attending inspections
- Answering phone calls
- Scheduling appointments
- Showing homes
- Running CMAs
- Answering emails
- Attending training and pursuing continuing education
- Answering questions from others in the office
- Sending contracts for signature
- Preparing addendums, counter offers, and other documents
- Attending broker tours

Lead generation can be enjoyable when you find the ways to do it that work best for you. Below are just some of the opportunities to find new leads that new agents often miss.

### Your sphere of influence
- Current or former coworkers
- People you meet at open houses
- Out-of-area Realtors who need a referral partner
- Door-knocking in neighborhoods you've sold property as well as neighborhoods where you want to sell property and establish yourself

### Social events
- Realtor training
- PTA meetings at your child's school
- Your child's sporting events
- Rec leagues you participate in
- Book club
- Your gym

### Social media
- Commenting on others' posts
- Posting about in-person or virtual meetups
- Being a guest on podcasts
- Being a BiggerPockets member and participating in forum discussions

The idea is to let people know you're an agent and will be there to help them when the time arises. Pretty much anything can be a lead-generation opportunity if you are able to meet people, build rapport, and talk about real estate.

Lead generation is not just a skill—it's the *most important* skill to have as a real estate agent. That's because lead generation is the only skill that will put people into the top of your funnel. Without it, all your other knowledge and efforts are useless. The good news is that, as with any skill, you can learn, develop, and ultimately master it. Later in this chapter I'll share sales, conversation, and psychological techniques to use at these types of events so you can begin the process of moving people along the sales funnel.

First, you'll need to learn to incorporate lead generation into your daily life. Agents are always working. Always. We don't pass up opportunities to find new people just because we are not in the office or on the clock. I find new leads most efficiently in non-work-related environments. Barbecues, sporting events, holiday parties, and other social gatherings are some of the best places to generate leads.

Because agents are always working, burnout is a real threat. If you want to maintain the level of interaction you'll need to be successful in this field, you must learn how to have fun while you work. Attending events like those listed in the previous paragraph allows you to have fun while you work. It will also help you avoid burnout!

For now, start thinking of ways you can train your brain to recognize these opportunities and their potential value to your business. The following are essential to successful lead generation:

- Consistency
- Credibility
- Clarity
- Conciseness
- The law of reciprocity

## Consistency

If lead generation isn't consistent, it's not of much use. Most people won't send you a referral after one call. The point is to stay top of mind with those you talk to. Because a single conversation is not enough to keep you top of mind, you'll need to continually refresh your presence in the minds of those you talk to. Each conversation moves you from their subconscious into their conscious mind. With enough consistency over time, you'll establish yourself there, and people will remember to refer you future business much more frequently.

## Credibility

No one is going to vouch for you or send you referrals if they do not believe you are competent at your job. You want to garner a stellar reputation among the leads you are generating. Building credibility as a knowledgeable, professional, skilled agent is crucial to earning the confidence of those in your sphere of influence you will be relying on for referrals. Having up-to-date market knowledge and an overall awareness of what people want in a real estate agent is a great way to bolster and maintain your credibility.

## Clarity

There's an old saying, "If you confuse, you lose." What you want from your conversations must be clear—this is essential. Talking to someone just to talk to them and pretending that's lead generation doesn't serve anybody. Conversations should be focused on relationship building and mutually beneficial exchanges. Make sure the people you talk to understand that you are an agent and would love to have them refer you to anybody needing to buy or sell a house. If you are unclear in expressing what you want, you are very unlikely to receive it!

## Conciseness

As your database of people to connect with grows, your time to connect with them will shrink. This is okay and a totally normal part of the process. Top producers get more done in less time—that is what makes them so productive. As you gain experience and skill, your conversations will become more fruitful and fulfilling—and in less time.

## The Law of Reciprocity

The law of reciprocity states that others will give to you what you give to them. It is an unspoken rule most of us abide by. The law of reciprocity is why we smile at people who smile at us and look to help those who helped us when we needed it most. Most decent human beings will have a hard time not repaying any good deed you do for them as long as they have a clear understanding of what you want (hence clarity). When engaging in lead generation, always look for ways to be of value and service to those you approach.

This will motivate them to return the favor and help you grow your business. It will also help avoid the seedy feeling we get when asking for something of someone we haven't given to first. All new agents are told to focus on lead generation. Few do it because asking someone for referrals to grow a business feels unnatural and selfish *if* you haven't given them anything first.

The best referrals come from people in your sphere. It's easier to get referrals from these people once you have helped them, so focus on how you can assist them with reaching their goals and solving their problems in a genuine way.

A great guide to doing this effectively is Gary Chapman's book *The 5 Love Languages*. This resource will help you understand how others receive love and how it may differ from the way you do. Another excellent resource is Dale Carnegie's *How to Win Friends and Influence People*.

## Tool Two: Appointments

While the first tool is all about finding potential clients, the second tool is all about securing them. A client is secured when they have signed an agreement establishing an agency relationship with you as their real estate agent. For sellers, we call these listing agreements. For buyers, we call these buyer representation agreements (or buyer-broker agreements). Different states have different laws and forms, so these will vary depending on where you live.

Having your client sign a form spelling out that you are their agent and they are your client cements the fiduciary responsibility you have toward them. It also ensures that they can't use you for your expertise and time and then have a different agent represent them in either the sale of their property or the purchase of the property they want to buy.

These forms protect the client because they spell out that the agent has a fiduciary duty to them and not a non-formal relationship. For buyers, an agreement can also include a guarantee that the agent will not ask the client to pay them a commission above what the seller is offering. For sellers, these forms establish the time frame during which the listing agent has the right to sell the house, what commissions will be paid, and how the agent is allowed to advertise the property.

In order to secure a client, I follow a specific process. While it's possible to informally ask a lead to sign a contract, you'll find this is not a good long-term strategy and often results in more work for you in the end. Asking someone to commit to you before you've proved your worth to them is a recipe for disaster. In the same way you'd never hire someone before an interview process or marry someone before dating them, it's foolish to ask a client to commit to you before they've been given a compelling reason to work with you.

I have all my clients sign agency paperwork before I commit to working with them, but I don't ask right away. The tool agents use to prepare clients is a presentation. You should have separate presentations for both buyer and seller leads. These presentations will be crucial to securing clients. In fact, the most important metric I use for evaluating my own business is the number of buyer or seller presentations I give in a week.

I give my presentations via a slideshow I created myself. Whenever possible, I hold them at my office and present them on a large television mounted on the wall. By asking clients to come to me, I establish control of the relationship and an authoritative position from the very beginning, and I suggest you do the same.

Establishing yourself as the expert is a crucial part of leading your clients down the sales funnel. Once you've worked with a few different clients, you'll see just how important it is that they respect your professional opinion and follow your advice. The process of buying or selling a property is incredibly nerve-racking and anxiety-inducing for most people. In order to keep your clients moving forward throughout this stressful process, you must gain their trust and respect. The presentation we conduct in step two is the best tool I've found for accomplishing this.

When I look back at every deal that has fallen apart on me, I see that failure could have been avoided had I prepared my client better for what complications to expect and how we would handle them. Clients back out of deals not because things go wrong but because they are not emotionally prepared to respond correctly when things go wrong.

The very best salespeople excel at this step, mostly as the result of serious effort. This is an extremely important skill to work on if you want to be a top producer. When new agents join my team, one of the first things I tell them to do is to learn to deliver these presentations naturally, smoothly, and with confidence. Successful completion of tool two will depend on your skill to win over and close your lead. This culminates in the successful signing of an agency agreement form.

## Tool Three: Psychology

The third tool you'll use in moving people down the funnel is your mastery of the psychology of human behavior. The better you grasp how the human mind and emotions work, the more successful you'll be at getting your clients into contract.

Top producers understand something many new agents don't: The home buying and selling process is largely an emotional one. There's a popular quote that comes up in sales training across professions: "A confused mind doesn't buy." This is absolutely true in real estate. The agents who put the most clients into contract understand that it is not their superior knowledge of real estate, but their mastery of human psychology, that makes clients feel comfortable moving forward.

That's why a large part of this book is devoted to understanding human psychology and how to apply it to real estate sales. Whenever you learn a script, an objection handler, or a specific way of addressing a problem, what you are *really* learning is how to use human psychology to help your clients understand the right move for them and see past their fears so they can make the best decision possible for their situation.

In the sales funnel, the most stressful moment comes when your buyer clients must decide which house to make an offer on and how much to offer, and your seller clients must choose whether to accept an offer for their home or make a counter offer and how much. Due to the high stakes for all parties involved, you will find yourself most in need of first-rate psychological skills during this stage. The quality of an agent's reputation is crucial to their ability to use psychology effectively. Top-producing agents are able to apply their understanding of human psychology to helping their clients because they are:

- Experts in their field
- Professional in their demeanor and communication
- Trustworthy and influential
- Able to secure referrals from their clients because they have created ravings fans out of them

## Expert

Top-producing agents know the market they work in and can easily communicate important information to their clients in a way the clients understand separates the top from the middle of the pack. These agents know how often houses sell, how long they sit on the market, how much inventory is currently available, and which neighborhoods are most in demand. They have at least a rudimentary understanding of remodel/rehab costs, how loans work, and how to protect their client's earnest-money deposits.

When people are in the presence of an expert, they feel safe, secure, and in good hands. It is easiest to control our fears when we are with someone who is in control and not scared or nervous. Being an expert agent requires you to be in control of your own emotions before you try to influence those of your clients. Expert agents are rarely scattered or shaken, do not speak ill of other agents, and can confidently come up with a plan of action to move forward when needed.

## Professional

Top-producing agents are true professionals and, as such, bring honor to themselves and their industry. While not every agent will always wear a suit, they will dress in a way that shows respect for their clients and respect for the position they hold, as well as the extremely important role they play in their clients' decisions. They communicate in a professional manner; their communication style makes their clients feel calm, well directed, and confident to proceed. Agents who show professionalism have a much easier job influencing their clients' important decisions and controlling their more unpredictable emotions.

When agents approach their profession too casually or without full commitment, clients will question their skills, advice, and guidance. Since a confused mind doesn't buy, it is important that agents keep their clients feeling confident and well informed throughout the process. While it's possible to influence your clients without a professional appearance, you'll have to work much, much harder to do so. If your clients can tell you take your role, your appearance, and your responsibility seriously, they are much more likely to take your guidance seriously!

## Trustworthy and Influential

Being trustworthy and influential go hand in hand. As someone who is exercising a large degree of influence over a huge financial decision for your clients, it is extremely important you be trustworthy. As Uncle Ben once told Peter Parker, "With great power comes great responsibility."

Trustworthy agents under-promise and over-deliver. They are aware of their clients' emotional state and know what to do to improve it. Trustworthy agents always tell the truth, never fudge numbers, and address their clients' questions and fears. When they do not know the answer to a question, they admit as much and look for the answer.

Influential agents exercise a degree of control over how their clients experience the process of buying or selling a home and use their experience, knowledge, and insight to help their clients make good decisions in uncertain times. Your clients *will* experience massive amounts of anxiety as a natural by-product of the uncertainty inherent to the process. Having the ability to influence the emotions of your clients is absolutely crucial—especially when you have a large number of clients looking to buy or sell a home. A firm grasp on human psychology will make your job much, much easier.

## Raving Fans

Doing a good job on a transaction is important, especially because you have a fiduciary responsibility to your clients. But you'll never have a growing, thriving business until you're able to do *more* than just a good job. Elite agents create raving fans out of their clients and receive a large number of referrals as a result. It is the cheapest, most effective form of lead generation out there.

If you want to take home a great profit for the year, you will need to create raving fans. Think of them as employees who work for you, sending you more business! This is an incredibly underrated but important part of building a solid real estate business. Many agents enter the profession looking for the secret nobody else knows—online portal leads, fancy search engine optimization platforms, paying for FSBO or expired leads. However, in my experience, there is absolutely no better lead than one who's been referred by a raving fan.

Consider these two scenarios:

## Scenario A

You pay several hundred dollars for an online lead that's been sold to two other agents. You are forced to call the lead within seconds of it coming in, then must compete with the two other agents, who are doing the same. Furthermore, the "lead" you are calling never wanted to work with you or any other agent in the first place and only wanted to ask questions about a specific property. You must contact them rapidly and repeatedly while under massive pressure to quickly build rapport before your competition does—and that's only for the leads who actually want an agent! They do not know you, do not trust you, and only want you to do their bidding on their timeline.

## Scenario B

You help clients buy a property and become friends during the process. These clients recognize your professionalism, expertise, and trustworthiness and absolutely love you for it. These clients have a friend who also wants to buy a house. They tell their friend how amazing you are, explain how your process works, say they *have* to work with you, and give you a glowing review. They connect you with their friend via text. You follow up with the friend with a phone call and introduce yourself. During the call, you schedule an appointment to deliver your buyer's presentation and gather all their info to put in your CRM. Before hanging up, you tell them your lender will be calling them to start the preapproval process, and you get the information required to look up the houses that meet their criteria in their area. You have these houses ready for review before you meet them.

In scenario A, you paid for a lead, but you really just bought yourself a headache. Online leads convert at very low percentages. This is a lot of work for a very low return and an extremely difficult way to create a new raving fan. You enter the relationship without momentum, without credibility, and without loyalty.

In scenario B, you paid nothing at all. You also received a very warm lead with whom you've pre-established a large degree of trust and a strong amount of credibility (those raving fans are huge!). You were able to skip the first two steps of the sales funnel (people and leads) and go right to the step where you can convert them to a client in your first meeting. You were also able to get them preapproved before the meeting and will have a list of homes to go over with them. They may even want to see those homes right after they sign the paperwork and the meeting is over.

A raving fan will send you *strong* leads for the rest of the time they are in your database and you stay in touch with them. They are *the* most important element in growing a thriving business and operating as a top real estate agent. Always, always look for ways to build raving fans and never take them for granted!

## Tool Four: Knowledge

The final tool to master in the sales funnel is real estate knowledge. This is the tool you will use to convert escrows into closings—and get paid! Experienced agents have gained knowledge from solving the problems they've encountered in their transactions throughout the years. You can gain knowledge through your own transactions or by learning from the experience of others. For this reason, knowledge is the least impactful tool to master. In every real estate office, there should already be someone with more knowledge than you. This can be your broker, sales manager, team leader, or productivity coach. Knowledge will always be necessary to keep deals from falling apart, but it doesn't always have to come from you.

Common examples of using knowledge to save an escrow could be:

- Finding a title company that can get the appropriate paperwork signed when the seller is a business or entity as opposed to a person

- Finding a lender that can fund a purchase when the first choice fails
- Recommending lender-placed mortgage insurance (LPMI) as opposed to PMI when interest rates rise and your buyer can no longer afford the loan
- Recommending buying down the interest rate for buyers when they find the payment will be higher than they anticipated
- Negotiating for sellers to pay closing costs when unexpected repairs are discovered during the inspection period
- Explaining homeowners' association (HOA) restrictions to your clients when HOA rules prohibit certain activities
- Prudently using home warranty services to make repairs after the purchase when the seller refuses to make them
- Negotiating for sellers to pay more in closing costs in return for a higher sales price when buyer clients run out of funds.
- Negotiating an extension of escrow or contingencies when lenders, title companies, or inspectors fall behind schedule
- Proposing creative lending scenarios such as home equity lines of credit (HELOCs) or 80/10/10 loans to help your clients avoid mortgage insurance
- Using HELOCs to fund the purchase of the home your sellers want to buy so they don't have to wait for their current home to close to access the funds
- Accepting offers contingent on finding a replacement property as opposed to writing an offer to purchase contingent on the sale of your client's current property
- Getting permission from neighboring units to allow your clients to make changes to the property that may otherwise be restricted
- Negotiating the vacancy of occupied units on properties your client wants to buy so the client can use a primary residence loan instead of an investment property loan (with a higher interest rate and down payment)
- Wisely proposing a request for repairs in a way that does not anger the seller
- Having sellers look at inspection reports before writing offers so they can review them while in a more reasonable frame of mind

This is only a small sample of things top producers do to solve problems that arise during escrow. That's why experience matters. The more you know about how the process of a home sale works, the more tools you'll have at your disposal to solve any problems that come up. You'll need these tools to keep your escrows closing.

Another major benefit to having a solid foundation of real estate knowledge is the ability to foresee potential problems and prevent them from happening in the first place. Having been the top producer in my office for my first four years as a full-time agent, I've had a lot more experience than the other agents. This has led to me creating systems that are much tighter than those of my peers, and the end result is a conversion ratio significantly higher than theirs.

I've learned what makes deals fall apart in escrow because I've seen it happen. Now I take extra precautions to prevent that from happening. Before I accept an offer on one of my listings, I call the lender for the buyers and make sure they have turned in current and up-to-date financial documents. I also have my sellers pay for a home inspection report to provide to the buyers *before* they write their offer. This has a huge impact on the number of credits the buyers are able to negotiate once we are in escrow. These are just to illustrate how growing in real estate knowledge will not only give you the tools to put out fires but will also help create systems to avoid those fires in the first place.

Agents with a strong knowledge base understand the importance of win-win solutions and focus on seeking them first. It can feel good for the ego to crush the other side when the chips are stacked in your favor. However, this often results in bigger problems later when the other side looks for ways to do the same to your clients. Some common examples of win-win solutions I've learned over the years are:

- Offering the sellers a higher purchase price in exchange for having them pay for my clients' closing costs. This allows clients with less money in the bank to feel more comfortable moving forward.
- Asking for a credit for repairs when unexpected damage is discovered through inspections.
- Asking sellers which repairs from the inspection report they are willing to make themselves or have a handyman handle for them. This way they only have to pay a credit for the items they choose not to fix.

- Offering to pay a token amount over the appraised price when a listing my buyers are trying to buy appraises low. This gets my clients a better price while allowing the sellers to save face and not feel taken advantage of.
- Submitting offers with appraisal contingencies in competitive markets with the addendum "buyer to pay up to X amount of dollars over the appraised price, not to exceed the purchase price." This gives both sides a much better idea how much money they will be receiving/spending up front, before the escrow opens and nerves escalate.
- Offering the seller of occupied property more money than we originally verbally agreed to so they can pay the tenants to leave and deliver a vacant property (cash for keys). This is cheaper for the buyers than an eviction and less risky for them as well, in addition to being more lucrative for the sellers.
- Having the sellers pay for one year of a home warranty plan for the buyers. This protects the sellers from being sued by the buyers if something unexpectedly breaks, because the buyers will be more likely to call the home warranty company for a replacement than to open a case in small claims court.
- Offer the sellers a free or reduced-cost rent-back agreement when they need it in cases where the buyers are currently in a lease they would have to break to occupy the new home. This saves the buyers money they would have to pay on their current lease and saves the sellers from having to find a short-term rental.

When an agent has a strong knowledge base, they can also set appropriate expectations for their clients. Miscommunicated expectations are the No. 1 reason relationships break down, as well as one of the biggest reasons escrows fall apart. If a buyer has an unrealistic expectation for how the inspection report will read, they are much more likely to overreact and back out of the deal or ask for unreasonable credits for repairs/reduction in purchase price. Knowledgeable agents set these expectations correctly from the outset of the relationship with their clients. This allows them to keep properties in escrow all the way to close. It also allows them to build better relationships with other agents. Everyone wants to work with the agent who closes!

Knowledgeable agents know what is coming in a transaction and stay ahead of the curve. They meet their timelines for contingency removals, send notice to perform documents promptly, and take responsibility for running both sides of the transaction. On my team, my assistants are trained not only to make sure we are hitting our timelines, but to ensure the other side is as well. On our listings, we call the buyer's agent to make sure their clients are submitting loan documents, appraisals are being ordered, and disclosures are being signed. This increases our odds of catching problems before they happen and limits the mistakes I have to deal with from other agents who are not as professional as we are.

One of the best and easiest ways to level the playing field in a transaction when you are the less knowledgeable agent is to hire a transaction coordinator (TC). TCs monitor timelines, get forms signed, and often schedule appointments, appraisals, inspections, and walk-throughs. You can learn a ton from a TC, and much faster than you would on your own. When I was an inexperienced new agent, I paid my TC double the normal rate to have her explain to me what every form meant and exactly what my responsibilities were. This increased my learning curve and ensured that I avoided the mistakes most new agents make.

Finally, knowledgeable agents can have several properties in contract at once without feeling overwhelmed, stressed, or cranky. There is a wild rhythm to real estate sales. As your lead generation and presentation skills improve, you'll find yourself with a large number of clients simultaneously. Top-producing agents know all too well the chaos of having a large number of properties in escrow at one time. It creates stress for the agent, who has to deal with the problems of escrow—and for their clients who are often on edge. The stress from the clients often makes its way to the agent as well, doubling the worry the agent is carrying.

The more knowledge you have, the less stressed you will feel with multiple properties in escrow. The less stress you feel, the better your lead generation will be. You will do it more consistently, and you will do it with better results. When we as agents are overly stressed, we subconsciously do not want more deals. This is the worst place we can be as business owners. When you don't want another client or contract, it shows in how you communicate, your demeanor, and your eagerness to follow up quickly with leads. More knowledge will leave you less stressed and more effective at putting new properties into contract. This leads to much more money in the end.

An added benefit to having several properties in contract at once is the relief you will feel from your own financial burdens. Too many agents provide poor financial advice to their clients when they aren't making enough money and don't have enough properties in contract. You don't want to be in the position of knowing you should advise your clients to back out but not knowing how you will pay your own mortgage if they do. This pressure creates scenarios where you may compromise your integrity and professionalism.

The best way to avoid giving poor service out of fear you won't earn a commission is having more commissions in the pipeline! If you have more properties in contract and more clients looking for properties, you won't feel pressured into making bad decisions.

By increasing your knowledge, you'll also increase your skills. Repeatedly saving escrows from falling out of contract will sharpen your skill set for putting houses into escrow and clients into contract. Sharp skills mean less work for more money, which is how you improve your business. When you consistently have several houses in escrow, you know you are winning in business and on your way to establishing yourself as a top producer.

## Closing Mastery

When you master the tools of the sales funnel, the stages of the sales funnel will take care of themselves. In fact, as a new agent, *all* you really need to focus on is improving your tools and adding to your database (more on that later).

As you improve your tools and consistently move more and more clients down the funnel, you'll find yourself with more and more closings, which means more income. And thanks to the leads provided by your ever-increasing number of satisfied clients, the more people you run through the funnel, the more prospects you'll have to put in at the top. In other words, the sales funnel is not just a way of understanding your job as an agent—it's also a self-sustaining ecosystem! Once I grasped this fact, my entire view of my business as a real estate agent changed.

This momentum is an incredibly powerful part of building a successful real estate business. In fact, it's an important part of succeeding at anything in life. The best businesspeople always look for ways to make their job easier. Understanding how to do this in terms of the sales funnel will also make your business more profitable and ultimately more sustainable. Here is an example of how this works from a real-life perspective:

You meet a prospect at an open house, gather their information, and put them in your database. You follow up (tool one: lead generation) with them every month, and eventually they refer you to their sister who wants to buy a home.

You call the sister, have a great initial conversation (with scripts I will share later), and set up an appointment (tool two: appointments) to meet in person at your office. You build a strong rapport, learn about her needs, and establish yourself as crucial to realizing her dream of owning a home. You set the tone, show your professionalism, get a buyer representation form signed, and let her know you will be calling her to see which homes you can show her.

You take your client to see the homes that match her criteria, demonstrating your professionalism and expertise throughout the process. You answer your client's questions and provide a firm and steady perspective that leaves her feeling more excited than scared. You address all her concerns and keep her motivated (tool three: psychology). You find a home she loves, write a competitive offer, and successfully put it under contract.

During your buyer's presentation you explained how appraisals, loans, and inspections all work. As a result, the client is prepared for the emotional ups and downs of the escrow process and does not overreact. You keep her calm, confident, and optimistic. During the escrow, interest rates rise and your client calls you in a panic. You assure her that things are fine because her lender locked in her rate and she just forgot. You successfully negotiate a credit for repairs after a home inspection reveals the roof is near the end of its life and the sellers had not previously disclosed that. You expertly handle each round of problems (tool four: knowledge), bring the property to closing, and give your client her keys.

Your client is thrilled with the job you did and the role you played in such a huge part of her life. You take a photo of her in front of her new home, have that made into a canvas picture, and give it to her as a gift to hang in her new home. You are there on moving day to help her move her possessions and provide branded cardboard boxes for her to use. You meet her friends and family, who are all very excited for your client, as well as the new neighbors. Your client says positive things about you, and everyone there gets an excellent impression of your work, personality, and success at your job.

You get the names of all the people you meet during the move and follow them all on your preferred social media. Later, you call, email, or text them to tell them how nice it was to meet them and how happy you were to be included in your client's personal life. You tell them that is the way you love to do business and say, "Even if you don't have a home to buy or sell, please consider me your Realtor as well. I'm here for any questions you may have about a property, interest rates, or the overall market. I love helping people, and everyone needs a professional to go to when they have questions about real estate. Let's make sure to stay in touch!"

These people are entered into your database and successfully become "people" (stage one) in your business. As part of your lead generation (tool one) you consistently check in with them and offer your help. In due time, these people let you know when they or someone they know needs to find out what their house is worth, how much of a loan they can be preapproved for, or what the state of the market currently is. You set up phone calls with these leads (stage two), set up appointments with them to secure their business (stage three), and start working with them to put them into contract (stage four), then close those contracts to earn more income (stage five)!

## Motivation

The critical last element of the sales funnel runs opposite the tools we use to move prospects to closing. This element, motivation, is key to the success of the sales funnel. As the saying goes, "You can lead a horse to water, but you can't make him drink." This is especially true in real estate. You can get people partway down the funnel using your tools, but if they aren't motivated to buy or sell a house, you cannot overcome this by applying more skill or effort. Motivation is the lubricant that makes the sales funnel effective. Without it you will find yourself frustrated, wasting time, and not making money.

There are many powerful tools, scripts, and questions you can ask to determine a person's motivation before committing to them. There's also a lot you can do to develop any hidden motivation already within them. To unlock your potential client's motivation to move along the sales funnel, you will have to address and calm their fears. Those looking to buy or sell a property often feel like they have two voices speaking to them. One, the angel of optimism, sits on their shoulder and whispers all the great reasons moving forward is the best option. The angel sounds like this:

- You're tired of paying rent to someone else.
- Real estate builds wealth more efficiently than anything else.
- Almost every wealthy person owns real estate.
- Owning a home will be one of the biggest accomplishments of your life.
- You want to set a good example for your kids.
- Interest rates may never be this low.
- Real estate is a terrific hedge against inflation.
- You need a tax write-off.
- Don't wait to buy real estate; buy real estate and wait.
- Rents are increasing every year.
- Having a place of your own will feel incredibly fulfilling.
- If you own real estate, you can sell it when it appreciates and buy more investment properties.
- Having a mortgage is like a forced savings plan.

The other voice is the devil of pessimism. It sits on the opposite shoulder and stokes the fires of their fears with every word it whispers. Most people will hear the angel of optimism much more loudly at the beginning of the transaction, but once the contract is signed, the devil of pessimism begins to take over. This naysayer whispers things like:

- You are going to be committed to a thirty-year mortgage. Are you sure you want that?
- It's nice to be able to just pick up and move across the country whenever you like—are you sure you want to give that up?
- Who knows what's really wrong with that house? Do you have enough money to fix all that?
- If you sell your home, will you find one you like more?
- What if you sell your home now and the market goes up later?
- What if you buy a home now and the market goes down later?
- What if the market tanks and you lose everything?
- Remember Uncle Jimmy? He lost his entire nest egg when his house was foreclosed on.
- What if the market corrects next month and you bought at the wrong time? What will everyone think?
- What if we go to war with another country and the economy crashes?
- Your agent did not pick up her phone. You're clearly just a commission to her.

- Did you really see every available home? What if there are more that you missed?
- Your agent may be holding out on you. He showed you only six homes.
- The market is already at its peak. You're a fool to buy now.
- The market is already dropping. Buying now is like catching a falling knife.
- The market has clearly bottomed out. Nobody wants to own real estate right now.

As you can see, there will always be reasons not to own real estate, and there will always be reasons why it's a great idea. That's why buying a home is so stressful! The bottom line? *You cannot create motivation in the heart of a client.*

Do not underestimate the importance of motivation in running a successful business. Your clients must have it, and you must have it too. Unmotivated agents rarely do well in real estate sales. Many agents who are very talented at using the tools I've described think they will be successful based on their talent alone. They won't. A real estate transaction must be fueled by motivation—the client's and the agent's—to reach completion!

## ➡ KEY CHAPTER POINTS

- The two jobs of every agent are to put people into the top of your funnel and to move people along the funnel.
- Sales funnel stages: people, leads, clients, contracts, closings.
- Sales funnel tools: lead generation, appointments, psychology, knowledge.
- Doctors, dentists, and lawyers do not provide their services for free. As a licensed professional, you should not do so either.
- Understanding how to classify the people who cross your path will clarify the course of action you should take with them—start building leads and classifying people you meet on BiggerPockets. com to practice!
- Understanding the tools needed to move someone down the funnel from one classification to the next will bring a clear sense of direction to your day.

- The keys to effective lead generation are consistency, credibility, clarity, conciseness, and the law of reciprocity.
- Setting appointments and delivering solid presentations is the best way to improve your conversion ratio.
- Top-producing agents strive to be experts in their field, professional, trustworthy, influential, and creators of raving fans.
- Although knowledge may seem like the most important tool to master, it is not. Knowledge is the easiest tool to leverage out and applies in the fewest situations.
- The more properties you close, the more money you will make and skills you will build to help put new people into the funnel and work them down.
- You *only* make money if you bring a prospect all the way from "people" to "closing." Bringing them 99 percent of the way there will earn you nothing.

## CHAPTER FIVE

# LEAD-GENERATION STRATEGIES

L ead generation is the first tool you will want to master on your way to becoming a top-producing real estate agent. It's not necessarily the smartest or most skilled agents who make the most money but those who are best at generating leads. This chapter will focus on how to generate leads effectively and in large numbers. There is no one-size-fits-all approach to lead generation. Every agent is different, and not every strategy will work for every agent.

I've said it before and I'll say it again—any and all agents need to check out BiggerPockets.com. The Premium membership is geared especially to real estate agents and will help you create a company profile, network with potential clients, and start off your lead generation on the right foot. If you're not yet ready for a Premium membership, you can still sign up for the site for free and then upgrade when you kick off your business! Check it out at BiggerPockets.com/Premium.

Next, I would advise you to try all the methods in this chapter and see which are the most effective for you. One thing that makes real estate sales so fun is the creativity involved in finding leads—there is *always* something you can be doing to locate leads while living your ideal life.

# Sphere of Influence

Generating leads within your sphere of influence (SOI) can be one of the most frugal and efficient ways to grow your real estate business. If this is the only method you use to generate leads, you can still be extremely successful! Your SOI consists of everyone you know, have interactions with, or exercise any influence over. This includes friends, neighbors, family members, coworkers, those who follow you on social media, and past acquaintances.

Keeping in touch with your SOI and talking to them about real estate can generate business for you. In *The Millionaire Real Estate Agent*, Gary Keller explains that if you contact the people in your database thirty-three times each year, you can expect to receive two referrals for every twelve people in your database. These contacts are referred to as "touches," and Gary's system is referred to as the 33 Touch. This is the first system I adopted as a new real estate agent, and it led to my being the top producer in my office in my first full-time year. In fact, 100 percent of the leads I generated in that first year came directly from my SOI and open houses—nothing else.

## High-Touch SOI Campaign

My personal variation on Gary's strategy involves more than thirty-three touches in a year and is as follows:

- 12 social media likes
- 12 social media comments
- 4 emails
- 1 personal handwritten note
- 1 birthday acknowledgment
- 1 yearly text on the anniversary of buying their home (for past clients)
- 4 invitations to meetups, client appreciation events, or other events
- 1 "pop by" where a small gift is hand-delivered (candy on Halloween, sparklers on the Fourth of July, and so on)
- 1 sports team magnet
- 1 yearly gift (such as a PopSocket for their phone or a chew toy for their dog)
- 12 market reports
- 12 newsletters
- Several text messages throughout the year to say hello

The most important reason for having a high-touch campaign is to ensure that your SOI remember you are a Realtor and will provide your name to the people they know who are talking about buying or selling a house.

## Keep Notes of Your Conversations in Your CRM

Your goal is to grow your database as large as you can and then systematically stay in touch with everyone in it. However, the more people in your database, the more difficult it becomes to keep your relationships and interactions with them genuine. Sheer volume makes it hard to remember what you talked about in your last conversation with each person. You don't want to ask someone how their job is going only to have them remind you that the last time you called they told you they'd just retired. To avoid such unfortunate scenarios, make sure you keep notes in your CRM with conversation details so you know where you left off with each person. This helps you to be a better friend and keeps your lead generation more authentic.

## Pay Attention to the Needs of People

You've probably heard that "people don't care how much you know until they know how much you care." The reality is that it's much easier for us to listen to what someone else has to say once we feel heard and understood by them. Keep this in mind during your conversations with the individuals in your database. Always make an effort to find out what is top of mind for the people you talk to. This also applies to those you meet at social or professional gatherings as well as people you communicate with by text and email. From there, you'll be surprised how many people open up very quickly and allow your relationship with them to go to deeper levels.

## Use Tags in Your CRM

In my CRM, I can "tag" members in my database with certain classifications, say, as members of meetups, investors, former coworkers, BiggerPockets fans, referral partners, you name it. These tags allow me to send relevant articles, blog posts, quotes, or other pieces of information to specific groups of people based on how I've tagged them in my system. This makes giving extra touches that much easier. It also allows me to make videos about topics geared toward a certain group and send that video to the group with one click. Using tags makes communication with your database much easier.

## Keep Records of Referrals

At the end of the year, I like to thank everyone who has sent me a referral throughout the year with a personal phone call or video. This lets my database know how much I appreciate them, makes future contacts easier, and rewards them with emotional gratitude for supporting my business. Sometimes I even send gifts to those who supplied the best referrals. This is only possible if I track each person who sent me a referral, so make sure you do the same!

## Have a Top 30

My favorite lead-generation strategy for communicating with my SOI is to have a Top 30. Your Top 30 will consist of the thirty most influential people in your SOI—those who are highly likely to send you referrals. The key to communicating with your Top 30 is simple: Assign a number from one to thirty to each person. On the day of the month that corresponds with their number, call that person and ask them, "How can I help you?" or "What do you need?" They might be an entrepreneur whose business could benefit from your support or a nonprofit executive who requires resources. Once you find out what they need, your job is to meet that need. By consistently contacting these thirty people and applying the law of reciprocity, you should get a high number of referrals coming your way.

## Bring Your SOI into Your World

The people you are developing relationships with want to feel like they know you and, more importantly, can contribute to your world. Inviting members of your database to share personal events in your life can be extremely effective. These events might include birthday parties, dinner parties, or graduation ceremonies—be sure to share these with your SOI as much as possible. When you have a baby, send a card with pictures to the addresses of everyone in your database and thank them for their support in helping you provide for your new child. They will love this, and it will create a much stronger connection.

## Plan Events

In my experience, planning events is a highly effective way to both deepen your connection with your database and motivate them to send you more referrals. Spending face-to-face time with your SOI and providing value through food, entertainment, or education is an excellent way to deepen your relationship with them. By sharing your sales numbers at some point during these events or, even better, sharing stories of clients you've helped, you demonstrate that you are successful at your job, which makes it easier for them to feel comfortable sending you referrals and strengthens your emotional bond with them.

## Marketing to Your SOI

For our purposes, "marketing" means "getting in front of." Some of the common ways you can get in front of your SOI are via social media, emails, texts, and newsletters. Social media is the easiest method. Make sure you post every time you sell a home or help a client for everyone to see. It's okay to send an occasional email with a listing for which you need a buyer, or if a buyer needs a listing you can't find on the MLS.

One of my favorite ways to initiate a conversation with someone and loop in the real estate angle is to text a picture or video of a home I was showing and say something like, "Saw this backsplash and immediately thought of you!" Finally, sending newsletters is a great and fairly simple way to share information about how your business, or, more importantly, the market is performing without putting pressure on the client to make time for a phone call or meeting.

## SOI Lead-Generation Scripts

The following are examples of conversations to have with people in your sphere of influence to ask for business or remind them that you are a real estate agent in low-pressure, comfortable, and genuine ways.

### Sample One: Sharing My Goal

The Sharing My Goal script is my bread-and-butter method for getting prospects to ask me what I have been up to. This lets me bring up real estate related topics in a natural way.

**Me:** "Hey, what's up, Jeff? It's David Greene. Did I catch you at a bad time?"

**Prospect:** "Hey, Dave. No, not at all. I've got a few minutes; what's up?"

**Me:** "Not too much. Was just driving by some tennis courts, and every time I do it reminds me of you. You been able to play much, or have the kids been keeping you too busy?"

**Prospect:** "Man, I haven't played tennis in years! Reminds me I need to get out there. I miss it."

**Me:** "Yeah, you were always really good. What's new in your life?"

**Prospect:** "Yeah, I wasn't too bad. Of course, the kids take up a lot of time, but I've got a fishing trip planned that I'm pretty excited about. Been a long time coming."

**Me:** "I bet! You're always such a hard worker. I'm happy you're able to get away for some downtime. You need it." (pause)

**Prospect:** "Yeah, so other than that, not too much. How about you? What's new in your world?"

**Me:** "Well, I've been getting into the gym again, and I just got my real estate license! I'm actually super excited about that. I've got a buyer I'm working with who wants a single story in Brookside, so I'm searching pretty hard to find one. Been walking the neighborhood, knocking on doors, and I love it. Best career move I ever made."

**Prospect:** "Wow, I had no idea. Good for you, Dave. Happy to see you found something you love."

**Me:** "Yeah, I really do. Almost as much as you loved tennis! In all seriousness, I love this stuff, so if you ever have any questions about the market, interest rates, what your house is worth, anything at all, please let me know. Just consider me your agent even if you don't have a house to sell. I'd love to help."

**Prospect:** "Will do! That's great to know. Always nice to have someone that knows the market."

**Me:** "Thanks! And keep me in mind if you hear of anyone who wants to buy or sell a house. My goal is to sell twelve houses my first year! Will you let me know how your fishing trip goes?"

**Prospect:** "Yeah, of course. Not sure if I'll catch twelve steelhead, but I'll do my best."

**Me:** "Okay, cool. I'm going to follow up with you on that, so every time you get a bite, just remember I'm going to ask you about it so you better have a story ready for me if it gets away!"

**Prospect:** "Okay, will do. Thanks for the call, Dave."

**Me:** "My pleasure, Jeff. I'll check in with you next month to see how it went. Great catching up!"

This script works in several ways:
1. It keeps most of the focus on the prospect and what he's excited about in his life.
2. It develops a connection between us, as I've now shown interest in what interests him.
3. It allows me to naturally bring up my real estate goals and ask for Jeff's help with them.
4. It sets me up for my next phone call with the prospect in a month.
5. It provides a way for me to broach the topic of real estate without seeming pushy, and subtly informs the prospect that I already have a client and business is going well.

If you use a variation of this script for the majority of your contacts, you'll find that asking for business is natural and easy.

### *Sample Two: The Quick Mention*

In this script, you quickly mention something about your real estate career and skills that make you look good, then change the subject before the prospect feels uncomfortable or "sold to." The goal is to plant a seed in their mind and impress them without making it obvious.

> **Me:** "Hey, Mary! Glad to see you again. When was the last time—summer of last year?"
>
> **Prospect:** "Oh wow, I think so! Time sure does fly!"
>
> **Me:** "Sure does! So, what have you and your family been up to?"
>
> **Prospect:** "Well, we spend a lot of time at our son's baseball games and he really likes Pokémon cards. Always trading them with his friends. Wheeling and dealing, that one is."
>
> **Me:** "I love it. I was the same way as a kid. Technically, I never really grew up. I just sold one of my listings for more than asking price in a hot market—just one reason why I love helping as many people as I can in real estate. So, between baseball and Pokémon, sounds like your son has a pretty good life. I think one of my clients used to coach the local college team actually; I'll see if he can get some tickets for you two to catch a game!"
>
> **Prospect:** "Oh wow, that would be so nice, David. Thank you for that!"
>
> **Me:** "It's my pleasure! You've always been supportive of me, so it feels good to reciprocate. I'll check in with him and let you know."
>
> **Prospect:** "Well, thanks. That's very kind. I know he'll be thrilled."

In this script, I mentioned two important aspects of my business:
1. I helped a seller get over asking.
2. I am working with more than one client.

Of course, in real life, your conversations will differ and will hopefully be more organic! But, in my script, I did this in a way that kept the conversation flowing and the attention on the prospect. I also found a way to work my real estate connections into a gift for her (baseball tickets). This will leave the prospect feeling like she wants to reciprocate, as well as remind her that I am good at my job and the best person to call when the time comes to buy or sell. When used correctly, this script will plant powerful seeds without arousing suspicion or seeming pushy.

### Sample Three: The Lead-In

Follow this strategy to lead the conversation in the direction you want it to go so that the client asks you the question you want to be asked. This keeps you from bringing up real estate on your own and appearing selfish or self-interested. Take this conversation with my friend Gina for example.

**Me:** "Hey there, Gina. Long time no see!"

**Prospect:** "Oh, hey there, David. Nice to see you again."

**Me:** "Yeah, it's been a really long time. What's new since the last time I saw you?"

**Prospect:** "Oh boy. Quite a bit! I got married, got into CrossFit, bought a house, and went back to school."

**Me:** "Holy cow! So nothing much, right?"

**Prospect:** "Well, yeah, it's been interesting."

**Me:** Purposeful pause.

**Prospect:** "So how about you? Anything new?"

**Me:** "Oh yeah! I got my real estate license and I've thrown myself into that world. Been studying contracts, listening to podcasts, reading books, and helping clients. I'm pretty good at it, and my clients are really happy!"

**Prospect:** "Wow, that's great to hear."

**Me:** "Oh yeah, it's fantastic. Let me know if you know of anyone interested in real estate—I'd love to talk to them. Where do you do CrossFit? Do they take referrals for a credit? I'd love to send any interested clients there, if it may help you!"

**Prospect:** "Oh, yeah they do! It's Mike's Gym in Fullerton."

**Me:** "Awesome! I'll be sure to have them tell the salesperson that Gina sent them then."

**Prospect:** "Thanks! You might help get me a month of dues waived!"

**Me:** "I sure hope so! Glad to hear you're doing something you love. The world needs more of that!"

In this script, we organically moved the conversation toward what was new in her life and in my life. This allowed me to mention my real estate career without seeming pushy or self-interested. I also tapped into the law of reciprocity by looking for ways to help her—and maybe get her monthly gym dues waived. This makes the prospect more likely to care about sending referrals to my business as well. When done correctly, this script allows you to bring up real estate in a natural way without engaging in a lengthy or deep conversation.

## Open Houses

Open houses are a reliable and cost-effective way to get yourself directly in front of those looking to buy a house. Remember, a "lead" is someone who wants to buy or sell a house and knows who you are, so meeting people at open houses is a surefire way to ensure you'll be interacting with leads, not just "people." When done with intent and skill, spending time at open houses can yield a great return on your investment.

There are typically two ways agents hold open houses. The first is when a seller agrees to allow their agent to hold their house open. The second is when a listing agent allows another agent to host an open house at their listing. Occasionally an agent may hold a house open that is not on the MLS, such as a pocket listing or a FSBO, but the majority of the open houses you hold will be for your own listings.

When it comes to holding your own open house, you'll need permission from your seller client. While some sellers believe open houses make it easier to sell their home, others don't like the idea of having strangers walking through their property. In general, I like to hold open houses for my listings, and I am honest with my sellers about why I do. These days, many buyers are likely to locate a property online first, and then schedule a time to see it. If the buyer doesn't have an agent and doesn't want to put in the work to find one, they will seek out open houses and stop by on their own. This means that holding open houses is a great way for agents to find new buyer clients.

Some agents tell their clients they will hold an open house to help get the house sold. While this may be true in certain circumstances, in general, you're unlikely to sell a listing to a buyer who is making random open house visits. It's best to be honest with your sellers about this up front and tell them it may be a lead generation tactic for your business. Some other potential reasons to host an open house include:

- Open houses provide you with direct feedback from potential clients and those who view the house. With this information, you can make adjustments to the staging, price, or condition of the home.
- Open houses help you gauge how much interest there is in the house and whether that interest wanes over time. If you consistently get lots of buyers showing up to your open house even as it sits on the market, that's a good sign.
- Open houses give you the opportunity to introduce yourself to neighbors and ask whether they know anyone who might like to move into the neighborhood and buy your listing.

In certain circumstances, holding an open house will not be worth your time and energy. Homes in less popular locations or that experience low demand are poor candidates for open houses.

## Open House Preparation

Once you've decided to hold an open house, your first step is to prepare for the big day. My team puts together a plastic container full of items the agent will need for the open house and places it in the trunk of their car before the weekend. Those items include:

- Open house signs
- A sign-in sheet
- Multiple branded pens and other branded materials
- Three picture frames: one for an MLS printout, another for a "Please Sign in Here" printout, and a branded team marketing flyer of the listing in the last frame
- A printout of every home listed as active for sale in the city where we are holding the open house
- A marketing pamphlet for buyers called "The Buyer's Blueprint" that details the homebuying process

Here are several things you can do to improve the results of your open house:
- Make phone calls around the neighborhood and spread the word about your listing and the date of the open house.
- Door knock the neighborhood and hand out marketing flyers for your listing.
- Advertise your open house on social media.
- Consider running sponsored social media ads.
- Add your open house information to popular listing portals like Zillow, Realtor.com, and Trulia.

These steps will increase your traffic and give you more opportunities for the face-to-face interactions that lead to finding new clients. Always arrive at least thirty minutes early to give yourself time to put out your signs. Place most of your signs at major intersections in areas where drivers are likeliest to see them. I also have an eight-foot-high flag I put in the front yard to make it easier for drivers to find the correct home.

As you enter the home to set up, the first thing you want to do is turn on every single light, open all the window shades to let in as much light as possible, and make sure your seller hasn't left any valuables, such as jewelry, cash, or prescription medications, lying around. Next, empty your box and set up an area for visitors to sign in. Make sure the area is near the front door and easy to find; the kitchen is often a good location. Keep in mind that you may get early visitors, so you want to have your sign-in sheet ready and the house prepared on time.

Once you're ready for visitors, take a moment to prepare yourself for some commonly asked questions. You should definitely know:

- The square footage of the property
- The lot size
- The age of the property
- The bedroom and bathroom count
- The school district closest to the house
- Other comparable sold properties
- Any outstanding features, such as solar panels, upgrades, and lower property taxes

## Open House Execution

Once you've set up the house and armed yourself with the information listed above, you're ready to start meeting potential clients. The key to a successful open house is your ability to build rapport quickly and then convert those personal connections into one-on-one appointments.

I'll be sharing my system for building rapport in a moment. First, I'd like you to consider the typical psychology of a person entering an open house. When someone decides to come to an open house, they usually hope to be able to look at the property without having to talk to (or be pressured by) the real estate agent. But as a real estate agent, since houses are mostly not sold from open houses, one of the main reasons you are there is to meet new people. This creates a challenge: Your job is to make them *want* to talk to you and be open to what you have to say.

When someone first walks in the front door, my advice is to proceed as follows:

1. Immediately introduce yourself, move toward them, and shake their hand while welcoming them inside.
2. Invite them into the home and ask them to please sign in.
3. Escort them to the sign-in sheet and motion toward it.
4. Stand nearby and watch as they sign in. If they were planning to provide fake information or just scribble nonsense, it'll be harder for them to do so while you're right there.
5. As soon as they are done signing in, physically distance yourself from them. This will alleviate their anxiety about being "pressured" by you.
6. Open your arms as you point to the rest of the home and say, "Please feel free to take a look around. I'll be here if you have any questions or just want to talk about the market in general."
7. Let them walk away. While they're gone, check to make sure you

can read their name and contact information, then write small notes to yourself about what they're wearing or something they said so you can remember them later.

8. Give them some time to look around. You want questions to arise in their mind that they'll need you to answer—things like, "Was this bathroom remodeled? Is this bedroom legal? How big is this lot?" These questions will open them up to the idea of talking to you again.

9. After they've had some time to view the home, approach them with a very general question, such as, "Is this the first house you've come to see, or have you been looking for a while?" or "How does this house compare to some of the others you've looked at?" You want to initiate conversation without making them feel like you're trying to sell them on the house.

10. Listen to their answers and continue to ask open-ended questions to establish a conversation and begin building rapport.

11. Get them talking as much as possible about what they like and don't like about real estate. Use the property you're in as a jumping-off point.

12. Casually and quickly mention little facts about yourself while talking to them about what they like and see whether they respond with interest or appear irritated.

13. Once they've seen the whole house and backyard, move the interaction back to the kitchen and the sign-up sheet.

14. Initiate your hooks (I'll discuss these below).

15. If you get good feedback, continue the conversation for as long as naturally possible.

16. When you feel the time is right, prepare them for your next contact with them.

17. Offer to show them other homes in the area if they are interested.

18. Decide whether you should try to set the appointment right there or arrange another phone call first.

19. Thank them for coming, and let them know when you'll be contacting them next.

20. Confirm with them that the number and email they've provided are accurate. (You'd be surprised how often people change one digit in their phone number.)

Here are a few things to bear in mind about the steps outlined above:

- It's important that you initiate contact with confidence and boldness. This is the first impression the prospect will get of you, and you need to convey strength and assuredness.
- Once you've made that initial, decisive impression, it's just as important that you back away so they don't feel pressured, crowded, or defensive. Physically moving away and creating space will help them feel more relaxed.
- One big reason to hold an open house is to meet new clients and follow up with them. If you don't get their contact information, you've wasted your day.
- Escort them to the sign-in sheet and have them sign in. Remember, you are not obligated to allow them to enter if they don't sign in. You have put a lot of effort into setting up the open house. You've provided value, and they are, in essence, trading their contact information in exchange for that value.
- Once you've directed them to check out the house, try to listen to their conversations. Note any clues that will help you know when and how to initiate conversation with them and what kind of guidance they may be looking for. Some people want an agent who can help them decide what they want. Others already know what they want and just want someone to help them find it.
- Learn some details about them that you can include in your notes to jog your memory and help you initiate future conversations. Ask them what they do for a living, whether they have kids and if so, how old their kids are. This will help them feel more comfortable with you as well as give you more material to work with as you continue to establish a connection.
- Your ultimate goal is to build rapport. Everyone enjoys talking about their likes and dislikes. Use this information to get them talking and learn about their frustrations regarding real estate—the aim is to build trust here!
- Do not leave it up to them to contact you or make the first move. It's easier to avoid possible rejection by handing out your card and asking someone to call you, but that is not going to generate business. After you've made it clear that you have value to add and they can see that, prepare them for what comes next. Offer an in-person

consultation, coffee meeting, neighborhood tour, or phone call and see what they prefer.

- Make your notes on the sign-in sheet when they leave so you can remember to follow up accurately.

## Hooks

A hook is a piece of information that creates interest in the value you can offer a prospect. Used correctly, a hook is crucial to building rapport and is one of a real estate salesperson's most powerful tools. But beware: If you use a hook incorrectly, the lead will think you're being pushy and pull away. A bad hook is about you and your needs and repels the prospect. A good hook makes a prospect *want* to know more about you.

Trying to set an appointment before you've hooked the lead is like trying to reel in a fish before you've set the hook. They'll get away, and you'll be left frustrated. Each agent needs to develop their own hooks. The following are some of mine and why they work for me.

### *Has anyone talked to you about which parts of town have higher property taxes and which have lower?*

This hook is one of my best. Most buyers don't understand how property taxes work and don't know they can vary by neighborhood. By asking this question, you are showing that you care about their finances and can help them in a way they didn't even know they needed. It's a fantastic way to show your value and make them wonder, "What more does this agent know that I don't know about?"

### *Has anyone discussed with you how you can avoid PMI without putting down 20 percent?*

Similar to the first hook, this one introduces something most buyers did not even know was possible. It's called lender-placed mortgage insurance (LPMI) and usually involves a slightly higher interest rate in exchange for no mortgage insurance. The difference in monthly price is usually significantly better for the buyer's bottom line. This hook shows you care about saving them money, not just about your own commission.

*How much are you spending on rent right now? If you factored in the mortgage interest tax deduction, would owning be cheaper for you than renting?*

Many buyers don't know how the mortgage interest deduction works, and explaining it to them will showcase your professionalism and expertise. Once they see that you can provide value by helping them save money, they will be more open to hearing what else you have to offer. This hook can help get you an in-person appointment where you can go over this information in more detail.

*I hear you want to save up more money for a down payment. Have you looked into how much every $1,000 you put down will save you each month?*

Buyers know they want a low mortgage, and if they're in a fear-based mental state, their math might get a little fuzzy. This could result in them stressing over details that will have little to no impact on their bottom line. Bring them back to reality with the facts. At 3.5 percent interest, borrowing an extra $1,000 will cost the borrower an extra $4.50 a month. Conversely, putting down an additional $1,000 would save them only $4 a month. At 4.5 percent interest, that jumps to a whopping $5 a month. Use this information to do easy, fast math in your head when discussing prices.

For example, if a client says they want to save another $10,000 before buying a house, you can multiply $4 by 10 and quickly explain that this will save them a total of $40 a month. Is it worth saving $40 a month to continue renting for another six months and paying someone else your rent? What if home prices increase by more than that $10,000 while they wait? It's imperative for agents to understand the financial, and not just the emotional, side of real estate.

*It must be frustrating that you've written that many offers and never got into contract. Has your real estate agent sat down with you and gone over a strategy that will improve your odds?*

This hook makes it easier for you to get a prospect into your office for a buyer's presentation. If they ask what you mean, explain that before you help a client write an offer you do due diligence, including looking up other comparable properties' sold prices and building a rapport with the listing agent so you can find out how many offers they have and whether the buyer needs to be aggressive or can write a lower offer. Explain that you don't just "hope" your offer will get accepted—you write offers with the intention that they will be accepted. This shows that you are bold and proactive.

***What did your parents pay for their first house thirty years ago? Do you think they have any regrets when they see what their house is worth now?*** This hook gets them out of a fear-based mindset in which they worry about small details and into a broader, prosperity-based mindset in which they realize what they have to gain by taking action. If you can help shift your client's emotional state from negative to positive, they are much more likely to want to keep you around as their agent. People remember how you made them feel. Make them feel confident with you on their side.

***Would you be interested if we could get the sellers to buy you a cheaper interest rate on your loan?*** This is a great hook that makes you look creative and shrewd. What you'll do is explain how a lender can buy down an interest rate by paying more "points." These points are included as a closing cost in the loan. Explain to the prospects that you like to write offers that are higher in price but include closing cost credits for your clients. That extra $10,000 in price is only $40 a month to the buyer, but if they get back the same $10,000 in closing cost credits, they can use the money to improve the property (and make the property worth more than the $10,000 they put into it in the long term), invest in more real estate at better than the 3.5 percent return they paid to borrow that money from the bank, or buy their rate down. If the rate buydown decreases the monthly payment by more than it cost to borrow the additional money, you've effectively gotten the seller to lower your clients' monthly payments.

***Do you know how long houses are sitting on the market before they go into contract?*** This one simple question opens the door for you to demonstrate your knowledge of the local market. By sharing the average days on market for the homes the prospect is interested in, you can help them understand whether they need to write higher or lower offers based on market conditions.

Use hooks to create interest in what you can offer your clients, then convert that interest into in-person appointments to move the lead down your funnel to the next stage of becoming your client. Open houses are great forums for practicing this.

Once you've completed the open house, you'll want to follow up with the people you met so you can get them into your database and start adding value to your relationship with them. For those interested in buying a home, you'll want to set an appointment to meet with them in person as soon as possible.

## After the Open House

I recommend taking the following actions after every open house:

- Follow up three ways with every visitor to the open home within twenty-four hours. I prefer a phone call, an email, and a handwritten card. I also use a personalized video at times.
- Call every person who signed into your open home the next day to thank them for coming, express your pleasure at having met them, and ask how you can be of service to them at this time.
- Set appointments with any willing prospects ASAP.
- Enter every contact from your sign-in sheet into your database. Include the notes you took on your sign-in sheet so you can remember who each person was later.
- If you have an open house follow-up system, apply it to the leads you just added to your database.
- Call the neighbors you spoke with before the open house to tell them how many people came, what kind of feedback you received, and ask whether they would like to hear what the house sells for when it does.
- Door knock the neighborhood and use feedback from your open house to initiate conversations to find out who else is looking to sell soon or whose information you can obtain to put in your database.
- Create a summary for the seller of the home that includes how many people came and what feedback you received on their home.
- Post an interesting piece of information you learned during the open house on social media.

New agents on my team are encouraged to hold at least four open houses a month. Open houses will help you build your database, learn about new neighborhoods, *and* find new buyers. They also give you the opportunity to meet the neighbors around the home and stay in contact with them so you can help sell their homes when the time comes. Other than your sphere of influence, open homes will be the very best way for you to find buyers and, sometimes, buyer-seller combos.

# Using Referrals from Other Agents

Many agents don't realize it, but other real estate agents can actually be a great lead-generation tool. In my experience, there are several reasons Realtors don't want to work with a certain buyer or seller and will look to refer the deal to someone else. Your job is to be that someone else! Outlined below are some of the reasons agents will refer out business, and what you can do to be their referral partner of choice.

### They Don't Work in Your Area

The most common reason for referring out business is that an agent doesn't work in the area where a client wants to live. Because I'm willing to cover large geographical areas, I had assumed that other agents were too. I was wrong. Many agents won't drive more than thirty minutes to help a client, and some aren't even willing to service clients outside the town where they live! Whenever you hear agents say something like this, pay close attention: You want those agents to know that you enjoy working in your area, will take great care of their clients, and would love to service their referrals.

In my market, it's standard practice to pay the referring agent 25 percent of the referral fee. This is one way agents can make money—just refer clients! Look for ways to network with and get to know other real estate agents in order to do this minimal effort practice. A free Bigger-Pockets membership or a paid Premium membership for agents is an excellent place to start! You can advertise yourself on the site to other agents (and to potential clients) and begin to grow your referral network.

Broker tours and regional real estate training events also offer great opportunities to meet your peers. When you attend these events, don't just show up and take notes. Look to connect with as many agents as you can and find out as much about their business as possible—many of them are likely already signed up on BiggerPockets.com.

Ask the other Realtors which areas they service and, more importantly, which areas they do not. When they say they don't service the area you are in, ask them whether they have any rockstar agents they refer to there. If they don't, volunteer to be that rockstar! Tell them how much their clients will love you and that you're happy to pay the referral fee you choose. Get their contact information and make an effort to stay in touch. You want to generate leads among these agents just as much as you do among potential clients. Check in with them to find out how their business is doing, how their sales have been, and what struggles they are having. Not only will this help you sharpen your own skills as you talk business with them, it will also keep you top of mind so they think of you when they have a referral in your area. Be sure to add them on social media and encourage them to add you. When they see your posts about closing deals, it will increase their confidence in you.

## They Don't Service That Level of Clientele

Some real estate agents have a very specific type of clientele they service and, even more significant, a type they do not. Some agents avoid all first-time home buyers, whereas others prefer to work *only* with first-time buyers. Some agents prefer luxury listings, while others are intimidated by them. Some agents specialize in investors; others want nothing to do with them. With all the types of clients out there, there is something for everybody.

A great lead-generation tool is to find agents who do not want to work with the type of clientele you do. If you like luxury real estate, look for agents who dislike it. If you specialize in working with investors, seek out agents who don't. Share information about the types of properties and clients you work with, and let other agents know that you want those referrals when they arrive!

## They Are Too Busy with Their Own Clients

One of the best problems in real estate is having so many clients that you can't service them all! When this happens, you may have to refer out new clients until you can either hire someone to help you or finish working with the clients you have. This is obviously most common among top-producing agents—which is an excellent reason to network with them.

Let those agents know that if they ever need to refer out a client, you'll do a great job and make them look good. When you check in with them to see how business is going and they tell you they're swamped, ask if there is anyone you can take off their hands or help them with. An effective way to get your foot in the door is to offer to show their clients homes or attend inspections for them. If you prove yourself trustworthy in a small way, top-producing agents are more likely to trust you later with the bigger responsibility of handling their referrals.

## Personal Issues Are Interfering with Work

From time to time we all face personal issues that prevent us from giving our best or even giving anything. Sick kids, bad breakups, physical injuries, family problems—any of these can lead to a lack of emotional bandwidth, making it difficult to help clients who usually need quite a bit of emotional support themselves. When an agent facing these types of challenges isn't able to take on a new client, you want to be their go-to person. Learn to listen for key words like "pregnancy," "divorce," "surgery," and others that indicate major change is coming, and offer your services accordingly.

## They Don't Belong to the Same MLS as You

If a real estate agent isn't a member of the MLS you belong to, they may not be able to service a client in your area. Personally, I usually find it worthwhile to pay the dues to join an additional MLS, but some agents don't want the hassle. If they don't know anyone in the area, they'll be forced to call other real estate offices and ask for their top agents; but if they know you, they'll just call you instead. Look for ways to be that first call they make! Prioritize talking to Realtors in other markets and MLS areas to keep a steady stream of referrals coming your way.

I've done this with particular success in my hometown of Manteca, California. I now live and work in the San Francisco Bay Area, which is only about forty-five minutes from Manteca but uses a completely different MLS. To most Bay Area real estate agents, Manteca may as well be another country. Because they know that I grew up and still work there, I've started getting all the Manteca referrals. This has led to Realtors telling other Realtors that I can handle all the Manteca referrals and basically made me the "Manteca guy." Become the go-to person in your market and a lot of business will come your way.

# Meetups

A meetup is an event where people with similar interests get together to network and discuss the interest they share. Some are formal, with a speaker and a specific topic, while others are informal social gatherings. Meetups are great places to get to know others who are interested in real estate investing and could become clients down the road. They are my favorite way to meet new prospects.

When I hold meetups, I organize, plan, and present at them myself specifically on investing in real estate. My first task is posting the meetup on event websites or posting it directly on BiggerPockets.com/Events. (This is where I get the most interest, typically!) I offer attendees information on how to reach their financial goals through real estate in exchange for the opportunity to develop relationships with them so I can represent them when they're buying or selling real estate later. These meetups allow me to do several things:

- Showcase my knowledge of real estate
- Develop trust, rapport, and connections
- Gather contact information to enter into my database
- Put the word out that I'm looking for people I can help with buying or selling houses

The best way to obtain contact info for your database is to require attendees to register via a website like Eventbrite. This lets you require them to provide their name, email address, and phone number in order to register. You can then convert this information into a spreadsheet file that can be easily uploaded to your CRM or database.

Running meetups will help you grow your database, strengthen your speaking skills, and improve your market knowledge. They also provide a great opportunity for issuing a clear call to action by asking attendees for their business.

Besides, spending time with people in person is always more fun than talking with them on the phone. Just remember: Don't leave it up to the people you talk to at these events to contact you. Always take the initiative to contact them! Your goal at every event is to leave with several new names, numbers, and social media accounts of people you made great connections with so you can keep building those relationships.

# Social Media

Social media has many uses because it gets so much attention from so many eyeballs. While it's great for marketing and advertising, it's also a strong tool for lead generation. Social media should be a fundamental piece of your high-touch SOI campaign and allow you to stay in touch with your sphere.

You can also use social media to showcase your coming-soon listings, pending deals, and sold properties. While you want others to see your business activity, make sure that's not all they see. A good rule of thumb is to keep 60 percent of your posts personal and 40 percent business-related. I recommend that agents post whenever they:

- Take on a listing
- Show homes
- Prepare for an open house
- Hold an open house
- Put someone into contract
- Have a client who receives the keys to their new home
- Attend classes
- Have a market update to share
- Have info on new real estate laws to share
- Receive an award
- See a funny real estate meme
- Get a testimonial from an excited client

There are several apps that can improve the production value of what you post:

- Word Swag is an app I use to add text to pictures of homes.
- Canva is an easy-to-use app and website for creating visually appealing content.
- PhotoGrid lets you combine pictures, such as before and after shots.
- Splice allows you to make short videos out of pictures.
- Reposter for Instagram helps you take content from other people's pages and post it on your own.

When posting about a specific real estate transaction, be sure to include details that explain what made it a win for the client. Did they get all their closing costs paid for? Did the seller get more than asking price? Did the buyer get a deal under the appraised value? Sharing these details makes a great impression and sets you apart.

# Farming

Farming is the act of claiming a neighborhood for yourself by building a large number of connections so you can dominate that particular segment of the market. The idea is that the more of your for-sale signs you can get into yards, the easier it will be to talk to people. The more people you talk to, the more listings you can take, and the cycle should continue with ease. Farming is all about momentum, which you establish by putting in consistent effort over time. There are two primary methods you'll use to do this—door knocking and circle calling.

Door knocking is exactly what it sounds like—you walk around a neighborhood knocking on doors and introducing yourself to people. Most agents do this before an open house, but you can do it anytime. Many agents like to bring a flyer or market report to pass out as an icebreaker, but that isn't necessary. What is necessary is your ability to make a quick connection, keep a conversation flowing, and build rapport with a stranger—then capitalize on that rapport by following up consistently so the neighbors don't forget who you are.

When you find someone who is especially open to talking to you, try to get them to invite you into their house and show you around. If you they point out features of their home they're particularly proud of, be sure to compliment them! Use this as an opportunity to ask them whether they plan on moving and what they most like about the neighborhood. Sometimes they will share knowledge about who may be planning to sell or move in the future.

As you build rapport, look for natural ways to ask for their email address or phone number. You can offer to send them monthly reports on the value of their home, neighborhood statistics, or what other homes are selling for. You can also invite them to meetups you plan on holding. However you approach it, your goal is to make a connection you can build on later. With consistent effort over time, you will come to look forward to these door-knocking sessions and visiting with people you've befriended in the past. The more listings you take in these neighborhoods, the more credibility you'll have when speaking with the residents.

The second form of farming is circle calling, so called because you'll use software that creates a radius around all the properties surrounding an address you enter and gives you the names and phone numbers for the owners of these properties. You'll then call everyone within that circle to introduce yourself and see whether they know anyone thinking of buying or selling a home.

As you make these calls, your initial goal will be similar to door knocking: You'll want to gather people's information to put in your database and add these new connections to your high-touch SOI lead-generation campaign. Make sure to enter notes indicating what you talked about during the calls. You can make many more phone calls than door knocks per hour, but the quality of the interactions and the connections you build won't be as strong. For this reason, you'll want to combine the two methods for maximum effectiveness. Build rapport while door knocking, develop the relationships while calling, then deepen the connection the next time you door knock. After farming an area consistently, you will start to learn the names of all the people who live there, and your conversations should become fluid and natural.

## Clients

It may seem odd to consider your clients as a lead-generation strategy, but they are actually among the very best. Clients, both past and present, will bring you more leads than you could possibly imagine if you work them right. Who better to recommend you than people who are pleased with your work? Who talks about real estate more often than someone in the process of selling or buying a home? These clients can become walking billboards for your business if you plan it the right way.

With current clients, I ask for a referral five times during the sales process. The timing of these requests is crucial. It's important that you choose times when clients are excited and happy as opposed to negative or anxious. Nobody wants to think of who to send you as a referral if they feel you just dropped the ball. The five best times I've found to ask for a referral are:

1. Right after they sign the buyer representation or listing agreement.
2. After the first time I show them homes, or after debriefing them following their first showing.
3. After I tell them the offer was accepted on/for their home.
4. When the last contract contingency is removed.
5. When the house closes.

In my experience, these are the very best times to capitalize on the law of reciprocity. During my presentations, I prepare my clients by warning them ahead of time that I'll be asking them throughout the process if they know of anyone else who wants to buy or sell a home so they aren't surprised when I do.

## Moving Day

Anyone who's had to move knows it's the worst! Most people aren't completely prepared on moving day. They're often disorganized, with boxes still to be packed and furniture still to be disassembled. They may also be dealing with people who fail to show up, and they may not have enough vehicles. The whole process is physically strenuous, chaotic, and stressful.

It's been said that moving day is when you find out who your real friends are, and that's absolutely true. If you can be a source of calm in the face of this storm, your clients will definitely remember you—and reward you with positive word of mouth and referrals. As I mentioned Chapter Three, when I was a new agent, I would show up on moving day to help my clients pack and transport their belongings. I hired manual labor to help me, loaded up the truck, and brought their belongings to the new home. This allowed me to meet their family members (and real friends) and solidified my relationship with the clients. I highly recommend this to any agent; it's very good for lead generation.

If you don't have the time or are physically unable to assist with the actual move, there are plenty of other ways to help out and shine! Stop by and drop off food and drinks for those who are working. Your clients will love you for that. If you can't be at the house yourself, order pizza and soda and have it dropped off.

If you are especially outgoing and sociable, consider throwing your clients a housewarming party instead. You can schedule a celebration to help them kick things off in their new home once they've settled in. Organize the event, send the invitations, buy the food and beverages, and get ready to meet all your clients' close friends and family (a great lead-generation opportunity). If you put on a fun event and everyone enjoys themselves, your clients will remember you for years to come.

## Closing Gifts

My team always leaves a closing gift for clients who've just bought a new home. We know that the day the client gets their new keys is the most emotionally charged moment of the whole transaction, and we want to make the most of that. The closing gift can be anything you want, but the goal is for it to have an emotional impact.

We bring a basket full of soaps, towels, cleaning products, candles, and decorations to leave with the clients. We also bring a large prop that looks like a key with my company logo on it to take a photo with. We use this picture to show on our social media outlets and in our newsletters. When we post the photo, we ask viewers to congratulate the clients on their new accomplishment, providing some well-earned recognition and acknowledgment to our clients.

When we first put clients into contract, the showing assistant takes a picture of them in front of the house. We then have that picture made into a large canvas photo, which we also deliver on moving day. These gifts help us make their special day that much more special and let them know our relationship with them is what's most important.

## ➤ KEY CHAPTER POINTS

- Fill up your funnel with lead-generation prospects. The more prospects you start with, the more closings you'll end up with.
- Your SOI is the cheapest, easiest, and best way to generate leads for your business.
- High-touch campaigns help you stay organized and systematic when connecting with your database and SOI.
- You are always working, but it doesn't have to feel like work. Look for new ways to find clients for yourself no matter what you're doing.
- Keep notes in your CRM to remind you where you left off in the last conversation with a prospect.
- Put other people's needs before your own, and they'll be more likely to return the favor.
- Reward those who send you referrals so that they continue to do so.
- Your Top 30 are the thirty people who send you the most business. Make staying in touch with them a priority.
- Sign up for a BiggerPockets Premium membership (and collect leads for your business!) at www.BiggerPockets.com/Premium.
- Open houses can be great lead-generation opportunities if you work them correctly. Be bold, likable, and decisive in your interactions with those who arrive.

- Use the open house lead-generation process to gather contact information for follow-up later.
- Follow up with leads after your open house and be sure to enter them into your CRM.
- Use hooks to grab your leads' interest and attention and make them more likely to listen to what you have to say.
- In-person gatherings like parties, meetups, or client appreciation events can get you valuable face time with leads and clients, helping keep you top of mind.
- Other agents can be a source of leads for you.
- Don't forget to ask former or current clients for referrals!

# CHAPTER ▶ SIX

# LEAD FOLLOW-UP

While lead generation is the most important skill you can develop to make money in real estate sales, lead follow-up is the most important aspect of lead generation to master. Top-producing agents know that the real money flows from lead follow-up. Bad systems (or worse, no systems), inconsistent effort, and lack of drive can create big problems when it comes to following up with leads. If you aren't going to follow up with your leads, it hardly makes sense to generate them in the first place.

Lead generation and the touches involved are like chops of an ax to a tree. You don't know exactly how many it will take to knock down the tree, but you do know that if you continue to chop away, you'll eventually knock it down. On the other hand, if you wander through a forest chopping once or twice at whatever random trees cross your path, you won't topple any of them. So why do so many agents approach lead follow-up this way? It's because they aren't used to a profession in which it takes such consistent effort to yield a result.

In most workplaces and professions, your result is directly tied to your effort. If you have an hourly job and work only half a day, you'll earn a half day's pay. Real estate is different because you can work a client 95 percent of the way down the sales funnel and still earn as much as if you'd moved them only 5 percent of the way down: that is, nothing. It's easy to forget we're not earning revenue when we feel we are making progress with leads, clients, and escrows. If you want to make money, you have to remain focused on taking the *next* step and not looking back at the steps you've already taken. Consider the following example.

> Imagine you've walked into a clothing store. You head straight to your favorite section and notice a sale sign. As you make your way to the rack, a salesperson approaches you. They give you the standard greeting: "Hello, can I help you find anything?"
>
> You give the standard customer reply: "No, thanks. I'm just looking." The salesperson walks away and you continue browsing. Ten minutes later you find something you'd like to try on, and you're excited about it. You go to the dressing room and discover you'll need someone to let you in. You look around anxiously for a salesperson to unlock the dressing room door.

Now, let me ask you this: When you need assistance, do you search for the person who greeted you? If you're like most people, you do not. Rather than look for the person you briefly met and have not developed a relationship with, you just look for the first person you see who can help you out. You don't care who contacted you first; you just care who is available when you are ready to try on the clothes.

Real estate works the same way. If you don't stay in front of that lead you met at an open house, they aren't going to track you down and make sure you get their business. They're just going to find the first agent they see and ask *them* to set an appointment to look at the first house they like. If you want the sale, it's your job to make sure yours is the first face they see. You do this by staying in constant contact with them. You do this with lead follow-up.

To maintain a system for consistently following up with leads and not letting them slip through the cracks, you'll want a CRM that lets you assign automatic plans to either remind you to do tasks or actually do those tasks for you. You can create your own auto plans, although some may come standard with the CRM. The idea is to create a system for follow-up reminders so you don't forget to follow up with leads. These reminders can be as simple as a weekly prompt to call the prospect or as complicated as a system of automated emails, market reports, listing alerts, and text messages. The following are several strategies I use to make lead follow-up easier and improve lead conversion.

# Tracking Contacts

In *The Millionaire Real Estate Agent*, Gary Keller and Jay Papasan share the results of their research on connecting with potential clients and how often to contact them. They found that when you meet an interested buyer, it is best to spend the first eight weeks contacting them once a week in some meaningful way. This will cement you in their mind as their agent of choice. Consider using one of the following touches each week:

- **Handwritten thank-you note:** Express to the client how happy you were to meet them and how much you look forward to being able to represent them.
- **Follow-up call:** Call to find out what has been on their mind and what real estate-related questions they may have. If possible, ask questions to learn more about what is driving their decision to buy a house. See whether they have found any properties online they'd like you to look into.
- **Free gift:** Mail them something like a calendar or a PopSocket for their phone or another small item of value.
- **Sample property:** Email or text them about a property you think may catch their attention and get them excited about real estate.
- **Marketing pamphlet:** Email or mail them a pamphlet or flyer that explains you, your team, or a personal side of your business to help them get to know you better.
- **In-person interaction:** Set up an appointment to meet them in person, say, for coffee or lunch, to deepen the relationship and help them decide whether buying is right for them.

# Low-Touch Nurture Campaign

As opposed to your high-touch SOI campaign, a low-touch nurture campaign is geared toward people you don't know as well and who may not want to be contacted as frequently. These nurture campaigns should have no more than one touch per month. Newsletters, market updates, and a few calls a year are all you need to run a successful low-touch nurture campaign. Someone who isn't particularly receptive to your contact attempts but hasn't told you to beat it may be a good match for this type of campaign.

## Listing Alerts

A listing alert is a list of properties meeting your prospect's criteria that you send to them on a predetermined schedule. You can set up listing alerts from your CRM or your local MLS to be delivered weekly, bimonthly, or monthly. You'll want to send a big list of properties available in the neighborhood where a prospect is looking to buy or the neighborhood where a seller currently owns. The purpose is to keep them apprised of properties selling in their area of interest and to make it easier for them to contact you when they see something that catches their eye or that they have a question about. This is something of value you can provide to both buyer and seller leads to keep them engaged.

## Market Reports

A market report is a summary of real estate sales activity in a particular neighborhood, city, or area. My CRM, Brivity, compiles information from the MLS and sends an email to my database monthly with the current average sales price, average days on market, listing-to-sale ratio, and the properties themselves that sold that month. It then compares these figures with last month's averages so the prospect can gauge whether a market is heating up, cooling down, or holding steady—and plan accordingly. Sending your leads regular market reports along with your headshot and website is a great way of keeping yourself top of mind with them.

## Lead Follow-up Criteria

When it comes to how long you should follow up with any individual lead, I say, "until they sell, buy, or die." While it may be natural to worry about upsetting someone by contacting them too often, the far greater sin is not contacting them enough and having them end up buying or selling with someone else.

Remember how you felt when clothes shopping in our earlier example. You may be slightly irritated by the presence of the salesperson while you're browsing. However, all that goes out the window when you need someone to help you try on an item you're interested in. At that moment, you are glad for any salesperson's presence and grateful for their assistance. That's how your leads will feel when they finally need help with real estate, so make sure *you're* the agent they think of when they do. In the meantime, don't take it personally when they don't accept your calls, respond to your messages, or seem happy to hear from you. They just don't have a need for you yet. All that will change when they decide to sell their home or find one they are interested in viewing. If you've been following up with them consistently, you're the one they'll call.

To facilitate the follow-up process—which gets more complicated the more buyer and seller leads you have—I've developed a system that makes tracking prospects easier. The system consists of three main components—CRM, whiteboards, and spreadsheets—as well as several other supporting pieces I'll share with you. The key to successful lead follow-up is organization and execution. You need to create reminders for yourself to follow up, and you need to make sure you follow up consistently.

## CRM Lead Follow-up Support

My first line of attack is my CRM and the auto plans I create. When I enter a new lead into the database, an auto plan is assigned to them that automatically reminds me to complete a series of tasks. These reminders are spaced out over a period of several weeks. When I've finished this series of tasks, I am prompted to move the lead to a new auto plan—often my high-touch SOI campaign.

### Open House Preparation Auto Plan
1. Add open house to MLS.
2. Add open house date to property profile in CRM.
3. Make sure the open house appears on Zillow and other relevant websites.
4. Arrange with office manager to borrow open house signs.
5. Create twenty-five open house flyers for guests.
6. Prepare an agent's box with all items needed for the open house.
7. Send email template to seller on "How to Prepare for Your Open House."
8. Call seller to remind them about open house.
9. Pick up open house box from office.
10. Circle call the neighborhood one day before the open house is scheduled.
11. Add all attendees to CRM.
12. Add open house feedback to the CRM.

13. Email all agents who attended the open house for feedback.
14. Call all parties who attended the open house and place them on "Open House Lead Follow-Up" auto plan.

## New Buyer Lead Follow-up Auto Plan
1. Contact the lead ASAP, introduce myself, and gauge motivation.
2. Fill out Buyer Lead Sheet.
3. Introduce lead to lender via email.
4. Schedule a buyer's presentation.
5. Check in every three days to see whether preapproval has been issued.

## New Seller Lead Follow-up Auto Plan
1. Contact the lead and introduce myself. Obtain address, reason for moving, and prospective timeline. Ask for pictures or videos of property. Ask how much is owed on property.
2. Run comparative market analysis (CMA) on property.
3. Send address to appraiser to get their opinion of value.
4. Set appointment with seller for listing presentation.
5. Prepare listing presentation packet (folder, branded pens, marketing pamphlet, CMA, branded book, printed disclosure packet, printed listing agreement).
6. Put seller's information and appointment information into my Google calendar.
7. Make sure I have listing presentation packet before appointment.
8. Call the day before the listing appointment to confirm appointment and remind seller to have a key ready for me.

At any point during these plans, you may find that the client is unwilling or unable to move forward. In that case, you should pause and repeat the needed prior step before moving on to the next one. The important thing is that every day you see the task staring you in the face, and you take action to move that client further along your funnel and toward the next step. A good CRM can help you do this much more easily than trying to remember on your own.

You'll also notice that the tasks on these lists are clearly defined and therefore much easier to delegate. My assistant performs every step in the above plans other than giving the listing presentation or buyer's presentation herself. When you systemize the steps required to be successful, it becomes much easier to delegate the tasks within that system, enabling you to handle more leads—and more clients—at a time.

# Whiteboard Follow-up Support

In addition to my CRM, I use a whiteboard system, which offers a simple way to track leads, clients, and escrows for the team. It provides a solid overview of the transaction, as opposed to the very detailed information contained in the CRM. Anyone on the team can see and grasp the information at a glance.

## Escrow Board

For our escrows, my transaction coordinator uses a series of whiteboards that track the following information:

- Property address
- Date of accepted offer
- Date earnest money is due by
- Date disclosures need to be received, signed, and returned
- Inspection contingency expiration date
- Appraisal contingency expiration date
- Loan contingency expiration date
- Planned close of escrow date

As each milestone listed on the whiteboard is met, my transaction coordinator circles the date to signal its completion. This way everyone on the team can quickly see where we are with each escrow, and the TC can answer questions during phone calls by simply glancing at the whiteboard rather having to pull up the file in the computer or the CRM.

## Client Board

We have another board, directly to the left of the escrow board, that shows a list of our active buyer clients and listings. We use a color-coded system of dots next to the clients' names to help us track where we are with each of them.

- A red dot indicates the buyer client has signed a buyer representation agreement.
- A blue dot indicates the buyer is preapproved with a lender.
- A purple dot indicates the buyer is actively viewing properties.

This dot system allows my assistant to quickly see and prioritize who needs to be followed up with. If a buyer has not signed a buyer representation agreement, the buyer's agent needs to be notified for follow-up. If you don't have an assistant, looking at this board daily can quickly remind you if you need to get paperwork signed, set someone up on a home search, or follow up with the listing agent on an offer you wrote a few days ago. It can also remind you which buyers you're working with and where you are with them, what you did last, and what you need to follow up on today.

Next to the list of my active buyers is a list of my active listings. I track these on the same board so I can see which of my properties are not under contract and which seller clients I may need to send information or give an update to or touch base with. Some agents contact sellers once a week; others wait for the seller to contact them unless they have something specific to share.

The benefit of whiteboard tracking is that when you look at someone's address, it jogs your memory so that not only do you remember the piece of client information you randomly thought of at 2 a.m. but you actually send it to them! The human brain is terrible at storing large amounts of complex information. Getting all those details out of your head and onto a whiteboard is by far the most efficient way of staying on top of things.

## Lead Board

A lead board should be divided into three categories: nurtures, active leads, and ready for presentations. Nurtures are leads who have expressed interest in buying or selling but are not very motivated. They do not respond to all your messages, have not committed to working with you, and do not have a strong connection with you.

Active leads are those who have expressed strong interest in buying or selling a home but have not yet made an appointment to meet with you in person. These could be people you met at an open house, referrals from other agents, or friends who have told you they want to buy a house but aren't preapproved.

Those who are ready for presentations are the buyers or sellers who have agreed to meet with you but have not done so yet. These are typically the most motivated of all your leads and won't stay in this category for long, as they are almost clients. I make the agents on my team track all their leads on a whiteboard for the entire staff to see for several reasons:

- I want everyone else to see how hard each agent is working on lead generating. If an agent is not making phone calls or contacts, this will be reflected on their lead board.
- I don't want leads slipping through the cracks. If agents aren't tracking them, they will be lost to follow-up.
- I want the agents to feel the reward of gratification when they move a name from one side of the board (nurture or active buyer) to the next (active buyer or appointment scheduled).

Whiteboards are a very simple, clean, and easy way to track your leads, making your lead follow-up that much stronger and more consistent.

# Spreadsheets

The final component of my lead follow-up strategy is spreadsheets. Spreadsheets operate similarly to whiteboards but come into play when there are too many items to track on a physical board. My team and I use a spreadsheet we call a lead board that consists of a system of tabs, columns, and rows to track our leads and communicate regarding them twice weekly.

There are several tabs on my lead board, which I have listed below. My team and I spend the most time discussing the "active buyers" tab; we use the other tabs for tracking people, statuses, and tasks we need to complete for each buyer. I rely on a combination of interns, assistants, and new agents for accomplishing the tasks in the tabs. Once we open a particular tab, we have columns consisting of biographical information, the address of a property, or an area to write notes about the last time a buyer was contacted and their current status.

## Buyer Leads

The buyer leads tab is where we track the list of buyers who have expressed interest in buying a house but have not committed to working with us yet. In order to be labeled an "active buyer," they must have attended my buyer's presentation, signed a buyer representation agreement, and been preapproved with a lender.

This tab has four categories/columns:
- Name

- Notes (what they want, what they are looking for, timeline, etc.)
- Last contact date and information
- Next action required

The purpose of the buyer leads tab is very simple: to track those who have expressed interest in buying so they don't slip through the cracks. As a new agent, I would look at this list every single day and find a way to add someone new to it as well as think of ways to follow up with the leads that were on it. Sometimes I'd send an article related to real estate or the economy that I thought they'd like; other times I'd send a link to a property I knew would catch their attention and open a dialogue. The vast majority of your lead follow-up effort will be spent on this tab.

## Active Buyers

The active buyers tab consists of all the buyers who are actively looking at homes and writing offers. I discuss this tab with my two main assistants twice weekly to determine who is making progress, who is stuck, and what adjustments we may need to make. Every buyer is unique, and it takes a lot of work to help someone finally get a home they love under contract. If you're working with a buyer and doing the same thing over and over—say, writing offers below asking price "just to see if it works" or "because there's nothing to lose"—buyers can run out of stamina and eventually decide not to buy or settle for something less than they wanted.

When looking at this tab, check to see if there are any patterns in your client's behavior. Are they enthusiastic until they get to the point where they need to write an offer, then get scared? Do they say they want to buy a house but never make themselves available for showings? If you can identify a pattern with your active buyers, you can find the underlying cause beneath it and then address that with them. This will have a big impact on improving your conversion rate at a crucial point in your pipeline—helping clients get into contract!

## Properties We Need

This tab was developed out of necessity when I ended up with too many clients looking for house hack potential or fixer-upper properties and there were few to be found. Interns on our team would search the MLS for potential house hack properties and then send those properties to the appropriate buyers. This saved me a ton of time and helped me find more properties faster.

We developed a system where we set up keyword alerts in the confidential remarks section of the MLS to notify us of properties that were likely to fit a house hack client. Words like "bonus room," "converted," "unpermitted," "in-law," and "income" were all highly associated with properties likely to have spaces that could be rented out but were not advertised that way in the public remarks.

I use this tab to help train new agents to locate specific types of properties on the MLS, guiding the system of "hunters" I've sent out into the wild to find me the pieces I need to put a deal together. As they bring these back to me, I can share them with my buyers and see who wants to write an offer on the properties we've found.

## Property Info Needed

This tab is what I use when assigning interns to look up information we need about a property. If you don't have administrative help, this tab will be how you keep track of the questions you or your clients have about specific properties so you can get them answered at a time that is more convenient for you.

These questions can range from how many offers are out on a property to specific concerns about an inspection report or item noted on the disclosures. We often look up property taxes, school scores, and FHA eligibility. It's important to keep a list like this so you don't forget that your client asked you to look something up and fail to get back to them.

If you are a reasonably experienced agent looking to begin building a team, consider finding a new agent in your office and assigning them work based on this tab. It helps them gain experience and confidence with doing research and talking to other agents, and it saves you time, which you can then devote to lead follow-up!

## Preapprovals Out

This tab is how we track our buyer leads who have not completed a preapproval. The baton can easily be dropped when a client is passed off to the lender. Sometimes it's the fault of the lender, who isn't following up with the lead. Sometimes it's the fault of the client, who hasn't completed the application or submitted the necessary documents. Often it is a combination of the two. Regardless, you can't sell the buyer a home unless the preapproval is completed. Use this tab to stay in contact with the lenders your clients are working with and find out what you can do to facilitate the process.

Ask the lenders what paperwork the client is missing and how you can help. Ask your client what you can do to help them with the lender. If the lender isn't returning their calls, call the lender and ask them to do so. It's in your best interest to be actively involved in the relationship with the lender, because so much of your own business is dependent on this point in the funnel.

## Support Products

In addition to the three main components of my lead follow-up system (CRM, whiteboards, and spreadsheets), I use several support products to help me stay connected with leads and give them reasons to contact me. They also allow leads to do things like search for homes or ask questions about properties they see when they want to look at properties for themselves and I'm not aware of a specific need they have.

### IDX Website

IDX stands for Internet Data Exchange and is software that allows a website to connect to the MLS. This is the same technology used by big listing portals like Zillow and Trulia, but is more often used by agents through a personal, branded website. My website, www.DavidGreene24.com, allows users to register through the site and then search for houses in the MLS. When users find a property they're interested in, they can request a showing or more information about it directly through the website, which links to my CRM. When they register to use the site, their information is automatically populated into my CRM as a lead, and an auto plan is assigned to notify me to follow up with them.

I also encourage my active buyers to use my IDX website for their home search. Doing so allows me to observe their search patterns—what areas they're looking in, what price range they're considering, and what types of homes they're marking as their "favorite."

This technique can also work with those who aren't active buyers. I put all my active leads on a search that comes from my website, and I encourage them to start looking at houses there. Once they do, I can also see what they are looking at, how many times they look at it, and when they're looking. If you have a lead who hasn't been responsive for two months and then suddenly logs in and starts looking at homes, that's a sign you need to call that person ASAP! No matter how you choose to use it, an IDX website makes lead follow-up easier.

## Writing a Book

Publishing a short e-book is a great way to gain instant credibility and showcase both your intelligence and your knowledge of real estate. The book should give a small amount of information about your personal background and center mostly on what you can do to help clients. Think of it as a supercharged business card to hand out to new leads that will capture and hold their attention.

Putting together a book like this is much simpler than you may think. Amazon has a publishing service that makes it very easy to create both an e-book and a hard-copy version. Amazon will store the books in their warehouse, and you can have them printed and ordered on demand whenever you need a new batch. Companies like Fiverr, 99designs, and Reedsy simplify getting a book cover designed and made available for print.

You should include information that buyers and sellers would not have known had they not read about it in your book. Some examples are negotiation techniques, home inspection information, local market knowledge, commonly encountered problems and their solutions, and key contractual elements. You'll also want to cover what a client should look for in an agent and what agents do behind the scenes that most people aren't aware of.

Having a book that you can provide to potential clients is a great lead-generation technique. Your book makes it more likely for leads to reach out to *you* when you aren't reaching out to them. If your client keeps the book someplace where they will see it often, this will also help keep you top of mind.

## Refrigerator Magnets

I know, I know. You just rolled your eyes hardcore. For years, real estate agents have used these tacky items as a form of business cards, and most of us saw them on refrigerators throughout our childhood. Why are they still so popular? Because they work.

If your goal is to stay top of mind with people, you want to have your face and contact information squarely in front of them. You accomplish this at a conscious level by making phone calls and sending emails and texts. You accomplish this on a subconscious level by getting your information someplace in the home where clients will see it often. For that, there's no better place than the fridge!

A variation on this technique that's worked well for me is magnets showing sports team schedules. We order the magnets, mail them to the clients, and follow up to ask whether they received them during our lead-generation calls. This gives us something to talk about and gets me in front of the clients' eyes for an entire year—a guaranteed way to get leads calling you when you aren't calling them.

## Hero Sheet

Your hero sheet is a one-page marketing flyer that showcases your awards, accomplishments, and client testimonials. The goal is to make it easier for clients to feel confident in choosing you over other real estate agents.

Whenever an agent or member of my SOI reaches out about another party who may want my services, one of the first things I send them is my hero sheet. It captures their attention and puts them at ease regarding my ability to do what they need done. When they feel more confident, they are more likely to call me to set up an appointment, or at minimum answer my calls when I reach out to ask for one.

If you are on a team, be sure to include your team's awards and production levels. If you are a solo agent, highlight things your clients have said about you along with anything else you do for your clients that differentiates you from the competition. Make it easy for people to choose you!

## PopSockets

A PopSocket is a small, circular handle that fits on the back of a cellphone and makes it easier to hold. As phones become bigger and bigger, they become harder and harder to hold. Many people appreciate practical products like this. It's entirely possible to have your personal brand and contact information printed onto PopSockets that you can then give away to your clients.

PopSockets are small enough that they can be easily mailed or dropped off at a client's house. You can keep them in your car to hand out at parties, events, meetups, or even when you have a great conversation with a stranger at the grocery store. My team gives them out at events I host, open houses, and after every buyer's or listing presentation. In fact, we include them in the listing packet I bring with me to every listing appointment (along with the book, the hero sheet, and the blueprint, explained below).

## The Blueprint

This is my name for the marketing pamphlet I use to explain the escrow process to buyers and sellers. I have one version for buyers and another for sellers. Essentially, it's a "blueprint" for how a transaction progresses and what goes on behind the scenes that our clients wouldn't otherwise be aware of. It provides an eight-step overview of the escrow process along with a detailed breakdown of each step.

The blueprint also includes information on my personal and professional background. It briefly covers my law enforcement career, my experience owning rentals and flipping houses, and my business philosophy, which is centered on "protecting and serving" the interests of my clients. My blueprint has a strong professional feel to it and is available in both physical and electronic formats.

As soon as you have enough information about yourself and your past sales to create your own blueprint, have one made. Hand out copies at open houses and give them away to any leads who cross your path. If you can include information that makes people want to know more about you or a specific aspect of real estate sales, you can increase the likelihood of them reaching out to you when you aren't reaching out to them.

## Marketing Videos

One more great method for connecting with leads is to show them a marketing video. These videos showcase what you offer as a real estate agent and create a connection between you and the lead in a way that makes them feel more comfortable with you personally. I use two different kinds of marketing videos: a cartoon "explainer video" and a professionally edited highlight-reel video.

For the explainer video, I paid a company $300 to create a cartoon that would match a script I wrote. The cartoon is cute, charming, and welcoming, making it easier for leads who don't know me to feel less intimidated and more excited to work with me. Why are videos effective?

Consider the following statistics related to video content:

- 88 percent of marketers assert that video provides a positive return on investment.[3]
- 37 percent of home buyers use video in their home search.[4]
- 90 percent of customers say videos help them make a purchasing decision.[5]
- Real estate listings with video get 403 percent more inquiries than those without.[6]

While these statistics are geared more toward listing videos, they still showcase the growing popularity of video as a preferred way of receiving content. If you want to be a top-producing real estate agent, excelling at lead follow-up is nonnegotiable. Thankfully, it is a skill you can develop by mastering the systems and methods that work best for you.

 # KEY CHAPTER POINTS

- Agents need to close on houses to make money. Unless a house closes and a prospect is moved completely through the sales funnel, you will earn nothing.
- Leads will not necessarily seek you out when they want to buy or sell a house just because you've spoken to them about it in the past; rather, they will go with the first real estate agent available.
- Staying top of mind through consistent effort will make you the first person a lead thinks of when they are ready to buy or sell.
- A CRM provides a detailed, systemized, and structured way to conduct lead follow-up.
- Whiteboards are useful for high-level, at-a-glance lead tracking. They help jog your memory regarding whom to call and what to say.

**3** Dave Chaffey, "Video marketing statistics to know for 2020," February 2020, accessed at https://www.smartinsights.com/digital-marketing-platforms/video-marketing/video-marketing-statistics-to-know/.

**4** National Association of Realtors, "Real Estate in a Digital Age 2018 Report," December 2018, accessed at https://www.nar.realtor/sites/default/files/documents/2018-real-estate-in-a-digital-world-12-12-2018.pdf.

**5** Matt Bowman, "Video Marketing: The Future Of Content Marketing," February 2017, accessed at https://www.forbes.com/sites/forbesagencycouncil/2017/02/03/video-marketing-the-future-of-content-marketing/.

**6** Shaina Churchfield, "Realtors: Want 403% More Inquiries On Your Listing?" July 2014, accessed at https://wakebrandmedia.com/realtors-want-403-inquiries-listing/.

They also reinforce the need to keep people moving down the real estate funnel toward a paycheck.

- Spreadsheets are useful when you have too many leads to track on whiteboards or you have more information to track than you can reasonably remember. They allow you to create tabs for different purposes and make it easier to elicit help from partners, assistants, or interns.
- Keep your lead board spreadsheet updated regularly!
- Support products like a personalized app or IDX website will make it easier for leads to follow up with you when they see something that interests them.
- Books, hero sheets, and marketing pamphlets such as the blueprint can help leads learn more about you and make them want to reach out when they are ready to buy or sell.
- Products like PopSockets and refrigerator magnets can keep you top of mind with your prospects and clients.
- Marketing videos are an excellent way to make yourself seem more approachable to leads and create interest in contacting you or taking your calls.

CHAPTER ▶ SEVEN

# THE FUNDAMENTALS OF REAL ESTATE SALES

In any field of endeavor, there is a set of skills that are considered vital to achieving success. We refer to these skills as fundamentals. To be a top-producing agent, you must master the fundamentals of real estate sales. Without them, you cannot be successful. Simply understanding how and why the fundamentals work doesn't mean that you've mastered them. You must practice them over and over, until you can basically do them in your sleep. As you learn the skills in this chapter, commit to practicing them weekly, if not daily. You'll know you've achieved mastery when you're able to perform them on autopilot.

## Writing Offers

When it comes to writing offers, you'll want to be not just competent but fast. When I first started, it would take me several hours to write just one offer; these days I can put one together in under two minutes. Once you get into the rhythm of writing offers, you'll be just as quick.

The first thing to understand when writing an offer is the contract itself. Most agents use contracts that are prepared and reviewed by legal staff. I recommend that you read through the contract and try to understand, at least at a basic level, what each section specifies and what protections the buyers or sellers have in the various circumstances covered by the contract.

Once you have a general understanding of the contract, you'll notice that the number of items that need to be filled in or decided on when writing an offer is surprisingly small. Of these items, a good chunk of them will often be the same or similar for every offer you write. You'll also need to gather a few pieces of information from your client to add to the offer before it's ready to be presented.

Offer forms vary by state (and sometimes even by municipality), so I won't attempt to cover all possible variations. However, most offer forms are fairly similar, so I'll use a California purchase agreement as an example. You can then adapt this information to suit your specific state's forms.

The information on any purchase agreement can be broken down into three categories:

1. Information that does not change.
2. Information that can be changed.
3. Information that will change with every offer.

On my team, we take a purchase agreement and highlight in yellow the sections that will be different on every offer. The sample purchase agreement below spells out the terms of the contract, and anything filled into the lines and boxes is added by the agent.

CALIFORNIA
ASSOCIATION
OF REALTORS®

**CALIFORNIA**
**RESIDENTIAL PURCHASE AGREEMENT**
**AND JOINT ESCROW INSTRUCTIONS**
(C.A.R. Form RPA-CA, Revised 12/18)

**Date Prepared:** _06/27/2020_

**1. OFFER:**
  **A.** THIS IS AN OFFER FROM _____ *Buyer Client Name* _____ ("Buyer").
  **B.** THE REAL PROPERTY to be acquired is _____ *123 Main St, Pleasantville* _____ , situated in
    _Pleasantville_ (City), _____ (County), California, _____ (Zip Code), Assessor's Parcel No. _____ ("Property").
  **C.** THE PURCHASE PRICE offered is _Two Hundred Fifty Thousand_
    Dollars $ _$250,000.00_ .
  **D.** CLOSE OF ESCROW shall occur on ☐ _____ (date)(or ☐ _____ **Days** After Acceptance).
  **E.** Buyer and Seller are referred to herein as the "Parties." Brokers are not Parties to this Agreement.

**2. AGENCY:**
  **A.** DISCLOSURE: The Parties each acknowledge receipt of a ☒ "Disclosure Regarding Real Estate Agency Relationships" (C.A.R. Form AD).
  **B.** CONFIRMATION: The following agency relationships are confirmed for this transaction:
    **Seller's Brokerage Firm** _____ *Seller's Broker* _____ License Number _____
    Is the broker of (check one): ☒ the seller; or ☐ both the buyer and seller. (dual agent)
    Seller's Agent _____ *Listing Agent Name* _____ License Number _____
    Is (check one): ☒ the Seller's Agent. (salesperson or broker associate) ☐ both the Buyer's and Seller's Agent. (dual agent)
    **Buyer's Brokerage Firm** _____ *Your Broker* _____ License Number _____
    Is the broker of (check one): ☒ the buyer; or ☐ both the buyer and seller. (dual agent)
    Buyer's Agent _____ *Your Name* _____ License Number _____
    Is (check one): ☒ the Buyer's Agent. (salesperson or broker associate) ☐ both the Buyer's and Seller's Agent. (dual agent)
  **C.** POTENTIALLY COMPETING BUYERS AND SELLERS: The Parties each acknowledge receipt of a ☒ "Possible Representation of More than One Buyer or Seller - Disclosure and Consent" (C.A.R. Form PRBS).

**3. FINANCE TERMS:** Buyer represents that funds will be good when deposited with Escrow Holder.
  **A.** INITIAL DEPOSIT: Deposit shall be in the amount of . . . . . . . . . . . . . . . . . . . . . . . . . . . . . . . . . . . . . $ _7,500.00_
    **(1) Buyer Direct Deposit:** Buyer shall deliver deposit directly to Escrow Holder by electronic funds transfer, ☐ cashier's check, ☐ personal check, ☐ other _____ within 3 business days after Acceptance (or _____ );
    **OR (2)** ☐ Buyer Deposit with Agent: Buyer has given the deposit by personal check (or _____ ) to the agent submitting the offer (or to _____ ), made payable to _____ . The deposit shall be held uncashed until Acceptance and then deposited with Escrow Holder within 3 business days after Acceptance (or _____ ).
    Deposit checks given to agent shall be an original signed check and not a copy.
    (Note: Initial and increased deposits checks received by agent shall be recorded in Broker's trust fund log.)
  **B.** INCREASED DEPOSIT: Buyer shall deposit with Escrow Holder an increased deposit in the amount of . . . . . . . . $ _____
    within _____ **Days** After Acceptance (or _____ ).
    If the Parties agree to liquidated damages in this Agreement, they also agree to incorporate the increased deposit into the liquidated damages amount in a separate liquidated damages clause (C.A.R. Form RID) at the time the increased deposit is delivered to Escrow Holder.
  **C.** ☐ ALL CASH OFFER: No loan is needed to purchase the Property. This offer is NOT contingent on Buyer obtaining a loan. Written verification of sufficient funds to close this transaction IS ATTACHED to this offer or ☐ Buyer shall, within 3 (or _____ ) **Days** After Acceptance, Deliver to Seller such verification.
  **D.** LOAN(S):
    **(1) FIRST LOAN:** in the amount of . . . . . . . . . . . . . . . . . . . . . . . . . . . . . . . . . . . . . . . . . . . . . . . . . $ _225,000.00_
      This loan will be conventional financing **OR** ☐ FHA, ☐ VA, ☐ Seller financing (C.A.R. Form SFA), ☐ assumed financing (C.A.R. Form AFA), ☐ Other _____ . This loan shall be at a fixed rate not to exceed _____ % or, ☐ an adjustable rate loan with initial rate not to exceed _____ %.
      Regardless of the type of loan, Buyer shall pay points not to exceed _____ % of the loan amount.
    **(2)** ☐ SECOND LOAN in the amount of . . . . . . . . . . . . . . . . . . . . . . . . . . . . . . . . . . . . . . . . . . . . $ _____
      This loan will be conventional financing **OR** ☐ Seller financing (C.A.R. Form SFA), ☐ assumed financing (C.A.R. Form AFA), ☐ Other _____ . This loan shall be at a fixed rate not to exceed _____ % or, ☐ an adjustable rate loan with initial rate not to exceed _____ %.
      Regardless of the type of loan, Buyer shall pay points not to exceed _____ % of the loan amount.
    **(3) FHA/VA:** For any FHA or VA loan specified in 3D(1), Buyer has **17 (or** _____ **) Days** After Acceptance to Deliver to Seller written notice (C.A.R. Form FVA) of any lender-required repairs or costs that Buyer requests Seller to pay for or otherwise correct. Seller has no obligation to pay or satisfy lender requirements unless agreed in writing. A FHA/VA amendatory clause (C.A.R. Form FVAC) shall be a part of this Agreement.
  **E.** ADDITIONAL FINANCING TERMS: _Seller to credit buyer $5,000 in closing cost credit_
  **F.** BALANCE OF DOWN PAYMENT OR PURCHASE PRICE in the amount of . . . . . . . . . . . . . . . . . . . . . . . $ _17,500.00_
    to be deposited with Escrow Holder pursuant to Escrow Holder instructions.
  **G.** PURCHASE PRICE (TOTAL): . . . . . . . . . . . . . . . . . . . . . . . . . . . . . . . . . . . . . . . . . . . . . . . . . . . . . $ _250,000.00_

Buyer's Initials ( _____ ) ( _____ )          Seller's Initials ( _____ ) ( _____ )

© 1991-2018, California Association of REALTORS®, Inc.

RPA-CA REVISED 12/18 (PAGE 1 OF 10)
**CALIFORNIA RESIDENTIAL PURCHASE AGREEMENT (RPA-CA PAGE 1 OF 10)**

Keller Williams, 191 Sand Creek Road, Ste. 100 Brentwood, CA 94513      Phone: (209)689-3131    Fax:       Untitled
David Greene      Produced with Lone Wolf Transactions (zipForm Edition) 231 Shearson Cr. Cambridge, Ontario, Canada N1T 1J5   www.lwolf.com

In order to fill out an offer efficiently, you'll need to ask your clients for the information you want to include and fill in the rest in yourself. In general, these terms will be:

- Property address/legal description
- Purchase price

- Escrow period
- Name(s) of buyers and sellers
- Date of offer
- Earnest money deposit/binder amounts
- Loan amount
- Inspection period
- Appraisal period
- Loan approval period
- The names of the title and escrow companies
- License numbers for the respective agents
- Brokerages for the respective agents
- Whether the offer is contingent on selling another property
- Any closing cost credits requested

The terms that will remain largely unchanged are typically:
- Which closing costs buyers or sellers pay for (county transfer tax fees, title and escrow fees, etc.)
- Period of time the buyer has to deposit funds in escrow
- Period of time the seller has to wait after delivering a notice to perform before action can be taken
- When possession will change
- Whether there will be a seller rent-back

In order to prepare yourself to write timely offers, you should collect as much information and documentation from your buyer clients as possible up front. That way you avoid pressuring your client for these items at the last minute while the listing agent is negotiating with another offer! In my area, we always submit a signed offer sheet, a preapproval letter, and a document called the proof of funds, which shows that the buyer has the money needed for the down payment.

To make your offer stronger, you may also want to include a so-called love letter from the buyer to the seller saying how much they adore the house, a signed copy of the disclosures, and a signed copy of any inspections the seller has made available. Providing this up front will show the seller your client is that much more serious about closing the deal. It will also demonstrate that you are a highly organized agent who is capable of handling the many complications that can arise during the escrow period.

I recommend creating a folder within Google Drive or Dropbox (or any other cloud storage) and making separate files for each client within that folder. Then place all relevant documents, such as the preapproval letter and proof of funds, within each client's file so you have them ready when the client is ready to write an offer. You can also store these files on your work or home computer, but you won't be able to access them remotely on demand. My team uses Google Drive's free cloud storage so we can get things done anytime, anywhere. We also store these files in our team's CRM (Brivity), where they can be accessed by all team members.

Once you've collected and stored your client's documents, there are a few more steps you can take to streamline the process. We write our offers on the California Association of Realtors (CAR) website; you should have access to similar resources or associations in your area. The offers then go out to our clients by email for an electronic signature and, once signed, are forwarded to the appropriate parties. In the rare cases where a client cannot sign electronically, you can print out these forms and hand deliver them.

Whenever my team gets a new client, we create a folder for them on the CAR site and put together a cover sheet, which includes all the client's basic information. The info stored on this cover sheet can then be used to automatically populate other forms in the same folder. This single small step is a massive time-saver. Once you've applied this system to your own clients, writing an offer—even at the last minute—will be a breeze!

The goal of writing an offer is to put a property under contract. While this may seem obvious, to many clients it's not. It's up to you to advise them from the outset on the importance of the offer and how to write it in order to achieve the desired outcome. Otherwise, there's a good chance they will be advising *you* on how to write it. Of course, the client has the final say on what property they want to write an offer on and for how much, as well as what terms they want to include, but it's your job to use your expertise to influence their decision-making.

Before writing an offer for a property, you should call the listing agent and ask them what the seller is hoping for. Don't assume that every seller cares only about price. Some sellers may need time to rent the property back from the buyers after the house closes, others are aiming for an "as is" sale, and still others would prefer to sell to a buyer they can relate to personally. The only way to find out is by calling the listing agent. This step is key to getting your offer accepted.

Some listing agents may be reluctant to divulge information on how to get the property under contract. They will typically reply, "I don't know what to tell you. Write your highest and best offer, and I'll let you know what the seller says." When you run into a listing agent who takes this approach, understand that it usually comes from one of two places:

1. The listing agent is insecure and intimidated at the thought of talking to buyer's agents.
2. The listing agent is lazy or busy and does not care whether you or some other agent gets the house.

The first is characteristic of a newer, less experienced, or less skilled agent. The second is a symptom of high interest in the property or low interest on the part of the agent. In either case, the solution is the same— you need to make the listing agent feel comfortable with you. You do this by building rapport. The following is an example of how conversations with a difficult listing agent should go in a market geared toward sellers.

**You:** Hey there. This is (you) with (your brokerage). I'm calling about your listing on (location). I have a buyer for your property and was hoping we could discuss the offer we are going to write to make it as strong as possible for your seller before we do. Is now a bad time to talk?

**Listing agent:** Oh, hey there. No, I have a few minutes. What do you need to know? The seller wants the best price possible.

**You:** Thank you! First off, your house shows incredibly well and was beautifully marketed. It's one of the few houses we saw that looked even better in person than in the pictures. Other than price, was there anything the sellers were hoping to get?

**Listing agent:** Like what?

**You:** Well, do they need a rent-back? Are they hoping for a shorter escrow period? Do they need an as-is sale?

**Listing agent:** Well, they don't want to give any credits and want the most money possible. I don't think they need a rent-back. I'll have to ask them. We never discussed it.

**You:** If you could talk to them and get back to me, that'd be great! You did such a great job marketing that house I'm sure you've got a ton of interest.

**Listing agent:** Thank you for saying that. It was a lot of work and I don't think anyone else recognized that.

**You:** Okay, well, we just want to make sure we write an offer that makes you look great as well as gives us the best chance of getting the property. Can you share if you have any offers in hand and what ballpark the prices are so I can make sure we are the most competitive?

**Listing agent:** We actually don't have any offers in hand, but I'm getting a lot of interest every day. Please write your best offer.

**You:** We will! I know this is the perfect house for my clients and I just need to help them see that. Once they do, I know they'll close. I want to make sure they don't come in too low and hope for a counter. They also want to make sure that if they write a strong offer they will have it accepted immediately without a bidding war and the anxiety that brings. I'd like to write you an offer that makes your seller so happy they take it immediately, and I need to work together with you to make that happen. Can you share with me if there is a price you know they would jump at?

**Listing agent:** That's a tough question. We haven't talked about that. It's only been on the market for ten days, so it would have to be strong.

**You:** Would full asking price do it?

**Listing agent:** Maybe. I'm not sure.

**You:** What about $5,000 over ask with shortened contingencies?

**Listing agent:** I would love that. I think the seller would go for it.

**You:** How about $7,500 over ask with short contingencies. If we got you that today, could you get me an answer tonight?

**Listing agent:** Will your clients do that?

**You:** I will talk to them about it. If I can convince them to do that, can you convince your seller to get us an answer tonight?

**Listing agent:** Yes, if you get me an offer like that I will.

**You:** Okay. I'm going to call my client and broach the topic. You call your seller and run it by them. Let's call each other back in an hour and see what we found out. Sound good?

**Listing agent:** Sounds great. Thanks for calling. Please get me that offer!

**You:** Great! I look forward to working with you and having a smooth transaction.

Let's break down the components of this approach that make it so successful:

- You flattered the job the listing agent did to market the property.
- You played on the fact that most agents are underappreciated to build rapport.
- You responded to their coldness with warmth and wore them down.
- You clearly explained you would work with the agent, not against them, to make them look good.
- You pushed them to give you an answer on what price their client would want, even when they told you they didn't know. This revealed $5,000–$7,500 over asking price as the sweet spot the sellers would be happy with.
- You came up with a plan for each of you to contact your respective clients and then get back in touch, making it easy for the other agent to follow your lead without feeling manipulated or controlled.
- You presented yourself as someone they would *want* to work with.
- You were pleasant but persistent and hard to say no to.

Once you know what price you can get the property for, you must help your client feel good about offering that price or find out whether the house is not worth that much to them. If it isn't, you can redirect your efforts toward finding a new property or write your offer at a price the client feels the house *is* worth to them. Either way, you will have saved yourself time and your clients anxiety.

To master the art of writing offers, do the following:

1. Practice writing offers until you know exactly which pieces of information need to be filled in and how to do so.
2. Learn which parts of the contract never change and which seldom change.
3. Get the information from your clients you will need to fill in the parts of the offer that often change (price, deposit, type of loan, etc.).
4. Collect all necessary documents (preapproval, proof of funds, etc.) from your clients up front.
5. Create an electronic file to store your clients' documents.
6. Use electronic signature software to save time.
7. Forward the offer and associated documents to the listing agent in one email.
8. Call the listing agent to let them know you've sent an offer and ask them to confirm receipt.

## Using the MLS

An MLS is a collaborative effort among real estate agents in a specific geographic area that consolidates the listings of all participating properties in one location.

As a real estate agent, the MLS is where you will:

- Find properties to show your clients
- Look up information pertaining to properties your clients inquire about
- Enter your own listings to be seen by other agents
- Run CMAs
- Look up comparable sales before writing offers
- Set your clients up to automatically receive information about certain properties
- Look up information about properties that have already sold

These tasks constitute the majority of the work you'll be doing as a real estate agent. Agents who are the most comfortable using their MLS will be more aggressive and confident when it comes to taking action and answering client questions.

Start by learning how to perform a simple search in your MLS. Each MLS has a search page where you enter the criteria you want to filter your search through. At a minimum, you should specify the following criteria:

## Status

This is where you filter whether you want to see active listings (for sale), pending listings (under contract), or sold listings (already closed). Most MLS search pages have several categories for each status (such as pending, pending accepting backups, pending short sales); choose those most relevant to your search. For a CMA, you would choose active, pending, and sold. For a buyer search, you would stick to active listings.

## City

Since most MLSs include several cities, select those that your clients are most interested in.

## Price

Choose the price range your buyers are interested in and approved for. For the maximum price, I enter their preapproval amount plus $5,000–$10,000. I leave the minimum price blank unless that would result in an overwhelming amount of search results.

## Bedroom Count

Enter the minimum number of bedrooms your clients need. You can leave the maximum blank unless you have to eliminate certain properties from your search.

## Bathroom Count

In general, you want at least one and a half bathrooms for your clients. If that isn't feasible, ask them whether a one-bathroom home works for them.

These are the most important categories to filter. Most MLSs will allow you to refine your search even further—something to keep in mind if you think additional information will be useful to your clients.

Once you've set up a search, you can handpick listings to send your clients via email or text. You can also send your client the entire filtered list of homes so they can review it and notify you of any that interest them. You even save your search criteria and set up notifications to be sent to your clients, as I'll explain below.

## Drip Campaigns

Drip campaigns are automatic emails sent out directly from the MLS whenever a property hits the market that matches the criteria you've set up for your buyer client. You can also arrange to have your clients notified when a property drops in price. Drip campaigns save you the time of having to manually search the MLS and email your findings to your clients each day. They allow for consistent contact with your buyer clients via an email that can be delivered at a specific time of day.

I recommend sending your clients a daily email that arrives between 5 a.m. and 6 a.m. It will be waiting for them in their inbox when they wake up, which gives them the opportunity to go through the homes you've sent before they are distracted by the challenges of the rest of their day. Assuming they review the listings and send their comments to you first thing in the morning, you'll then have all day to research and respond to any questions your clients may have about the properties.

In order to make drip campaigns effective, you'll need to prepare your client for what to expect and how to communicate with you. Tell them they will receive an email every morning with all the new inventory that hits the market as well as properties that have dropped in price. Instruct them to text or email you with any questions, and find out how they would like to receive your replies. Emphasize that they will see only homes that match the criteria they have provided you with.

If the criteria you set up for your client don't generate enough results, your clients might get the impression that you're not providing them with all available options and start searching for properties themselves. This can make your job harder, so be sure to let them know that if they want to see more properties in their morning email, you will broaden the search criteria yourself to generate more results.

# Showing Homes

The home-showing process is where you will learn more about your clients' personalities and desires, help them feel comfortable moving forward on the right home, and take your relationship with them to a deeper level. If you do not master this fundamental aspect of the business, you will find yourself struggling to put buyers into contract and retaining clients for any significant period of time. Showing homes takes up more time in the buyer's process than anything else you'll do. Learning to put buyers into contract quickly, efficiently, and consistently can take you from a mediocre salesperson to a top producer.

Showing homes consists of the following steps:

1. Finding the homes your client wants to see
2. Scheduling appointments to see the homes
3. Showing the homes
4. Debriefing your clients
5. Performing due diligence
6. Writing offers

## Finding the Homes Your Clients Want to See

In a buyer's market, finding homes to show your clients isn't as difficult as it is in a seller's market. There will be more inventory and less competition. The downside is that buyers may hesitate to write a reasonable offer because market conditions do not create a sense of urgency. Ironically, you'll find homes sell much faster in a seller's market because buyers cannot be as picky or take as long to make a decision.

Finding homes your clients will want to see is an art. You'll have to ask your clients lots of questions so you can learn to assess the available inventory through their eyes. In addition, each market is unique with its own set of challenges. In a hot market like the San Francisco Bay Area, showing only homes that have been on the market for twenty days or longer is critical to success. Anything more recent than that will often sell for well over asking price. In other markets you can take your time, but clients will want to see only houses that are completely upgraded or in the best school districts.

Consider asking the following questions to help determine which houses your clients will want to see:

- Are you open to a fixer-upper that needs cosmetic work?

- Are you open to changing paint and flooring, or do you need the house to be perfect and turnkey?
- Will you look at houses on busy streets?
- Which is more important to you: the quality of the school district or the quality of the house?
- Do you need a pool, want a pool, or prefer not to have one?
- What is important to your children in a home?
- When you envision yourself enjoying holidays in the home, what is the picture in your mind?
- On the spectrum of affordability versus comfort, where do your preferences fall?
- Is this a starter home, stepping-stone home, or dream home?
- If a house doesn't check every single box on your dream list but meets your basic needs, are you open to buying it and finding your dream home later?
- How much stress are you willing to put up with in order to save money?

## Scheduling Appointments

Once you know which properties your clients would like to see, look up the showing instructions in the MLS. Some properties are vacant, and you will be able to show them anytime; others are occupied, and you will need an appointment in order to show them. When an appointment is necessary, check the instructions to see whether you should contact the listing agent or the seller directly. Contact the appropriate party and let them know what time you'd like to show the home. Give yourself a minimum of thirty minutes between appointments and be sure to allow for extended driving time when applicable.

Try to show your clients more than one home per outing. A tour that covers four or five homes, saving the best for last, is ideal. I recommend showing the cheapest or least desirable homes first, to get any disappointment out of the way and give buyers some context for evaluating the better properties. This way clients will look more favorably on the homes you think are more appropriate for them and be more inclined to see them as their best options.

Once you've scheduled the visits, I recommend making separate appointments in your phone's calendar for each home. Within each calendar note, you'll want to include the home's address as well as relevant information you may want to access when you're out showing the homes. On my team, my assistant enters this information for the agent showing the home into their calendar for them. I have them include the following information:

- The address of the home, so I can just click on the link in my phone's calendar instead of entering it manually into my phone's navigation app
- The name and number of the listing agent, so I can call them if I have any burning questions or problems accessing the home
- The price of the home, so I can tell the clients if they ask during the showing
- How long the home has been on the market, so I can answer "How cheap do you think we can get it?" if clients ask during the showing
- The lockbox location, so I don't look dumb trying to find the key
- Any unusual or specific instructions, such as a pet that needs to be kept locked in a room or the code to a home alarm system
- The gate code if the property is in a gated community

Including this information in your phone's calendar ahead of time will keep the process of showing homes as smooth as possible and allows you more bandwidth to focus on the clients' questions, emotions, and concerns.

## Showing the Properties

Before leaving to show the properties, you'll want to pack a folder with an MLS printout of each home, a pen, bottled water for each client, and snacks. My team uses a branded folder with my company's logo on it. I arrive prepared like this to set the tone right off the bat as professional and prepared. Provide the clients with the folder and encourage them to take notes on each house they see and write down any questions they may have. This removes pressure from you to reply on the spot to questions you may not have the answers to.

Tell the clients which house you will meet them at and arrive early so you can open the front door and turn on the lights. Greet your clients when they arrive and allow them to walk throughout the house at their own pace and take it all in. As they do, pay close attention to what they say, what they notice, and the facial expressions they make.

People may feel uncomfortable sharing negative thoughts and feelings, but their facial expressions will give them away. Pay extra close attention to what author Robert Greene calls micro-expressions: extremely quick flashes of emotion that reveal someone's true opinion before they wipe the expression away to hide it. If your client recoils in horror as soon as they see the kitchen, noticeably slumps their shoulders and sighs when they see the backyard, or rolls their eyes when they see the condition of the "walk-in" closet, you'll know they are not pleased.

Do not try to "sell" the house to the client unless you can tell they like the property. If you notice the client is not pleased with the property, mirror their sentiments to build credibility when they feel you support their taste and preferences. This credibility is necessary when you find a house they *do* like, and you want to encourage them to move forward on it.

Don't be afraid to ask your clients if they'd like to leave early when they see something in the house that is a deal breaker for them. If the yard is too small or the neighborhood feels unsafe, let the clients know you think the house isn't the best fit and you'd like to skip it and move on to the next one.

When you leave a house, text your clients the address to the next house on the list. Try to arrive at the next house before your clients in order to give yourself time to find the lockbox and open the door before they arrive. Struggling to gain access while your clients stand by waiting is awkward and embarrassing.

When it's time to go, make sure you don't accidentally leave with the key or the lockbox key housing mechanism. My advice is to leave the key in its tray the entire time or keep it in your hand or a pocket. Before you head out, check that all back doors, garage doors, and sliding glass doors are locked and the lights are turned off.

## Debriefing Your Clients

Once you've seen all the houses on your tour, you'll want to debrief your clients. This gives them an opportunity to talk through their feelings and figure out what they like and don't like. It also gives you the opportunity to see what's going on in their heads and their hearts. Debriefs can occur in a comfortable setting like a restaurant or a coffee shop, or by your client's car in front of the last house you see.

Start with open-ended questions, like the ones below, and let the clients talk.

- So, what did you think?
- How are you feeling after seeing these homes?
- What did you notice after seeing several homes in a row?
- How was this different from what you were expecting?
- What did you like most about today?
- What surprised you most about today?

Then move to more pointed questions that help you understand what they are really thinking, and sometimes help them understand these things themselves. Examples of pointed questions are:
- Which house was your favorite?
- What about that house made it your favorite?
- Which other homes did you like?
- Which features turned you off the most?
- What caught you most off guard?
- What questions do you have now that you did not have when we started?
- On a scale of one to ten, how much do you like your favorite house?
- What would you have to change about it to make it a perfect ten?

End the debrief by establishing what comes next. If they like one or several properties, tell them you'll be doing due diligence and getting back to them about writing an offer. If they did not like any properties, tell them you'll be looking up more possible candidates and getting back to them when you've found some.

## Performing Your Due Diligence

Once you find a property your client likes, you should perform the research process we call due diligence before putting together an offer. The following are some of the things you should research and report back to your clients on to help them make the best possible decision about the home.
- Are the property taxes high, low, or average for the city the house is in?
- Are the school scores high, low, or average for the city?
- Have interest rates increased from what your clients were told when they were preapproved?
- How many other buyers have written offers on the property?

- Is the property in an HOA, and if so, how much are the fees and what are the amenities?
- Is the HOA in litigation?
- How much will it cost to rehabilitate the property to a condition the buyers will be happy with?
- Have the sellers already filled out their disclosures and can these be delivered to the buyers?
- Are there any inspection reports available to review?
- What are comparable sales in the neighborhood?

This information will help your clients make a well-informed decision about whether the property is right for them and, if it is, how strong an offer they should write. Skipping this step now will create anxiety later in the escrow process. It may cause your clients to feel you did not represent them well, and make them more likely to back out of the contract. Finally, once you've done your due diligence research, call the listing agent to find out what needs to be done to write a strong offer.

# Understanding Paperwork

Understanding the forms required to close an escrow isn't the most glamorous part of being an agent, but it's still fundamental to the profession. Each state has specific forms required to close a transaction and others that are needed to solve specific problems that arise in escrow. The following is a summary of the basic forms you'll want to understand in order to feel confident when representing your client.

### Residential Purchase Agreement (RPA)
This is your offer sheet.

### Seller Counter Offer (SCO)
A form used by a seller to counter an offer from a buyer.

### Seller Multiple Counter Offer (SMCO)
A form sent out when more than one buyer submits an offer on a listing. The SMCO lets the buyers' agents know there were multiple offers received, and it allows the listing agent to counteroffer simultaneously.

### Buyer Counter Offer (BCO)

The form a buyer uses to respond to a seller's counter offer.

### Addendum

Forms used to add additional terms to a contract or remove terms agreed upon earlier in the process. Addendums function as catchalls when no specific form covers the content the agent wants to include, change, or retract.

### Extension of Time Addendum (ETA)

A form used to request more time for one party to perform something specified in the contract, such as an extension of a contingency or a new close of escrow date.

### Contingency Removal Form

Forms used to "waive" the right to use a contingency (back out of a deal and recover the deposit). In some states these forms are not necessary because the right to back out of a deal automatically expires when the agreed-upon deadline passes.

### Notice to Buyer to Perform (NBP)

The form needed to notify the buyer that a certain contingency or contractual obligation needs to be met or the seller will place their property back on the market.

### Demand to Close Escrow (DCE)

A form required in most states to be presented to a buyer before a seller can place their property back on the market when a buyer is unable or unwilling to close on the agreed-upon date.

### Disclosure

Paperwork filled out by sellers "disclosing" known defects of the house.

### Seller in Possession (SIP)

This form was created to define the terms under which a seller may remain in the property after it is purchased by the buyer. It is intended for short-term occupancy.

### Request for Repairs (RR)
A form used by the buyer to request that the seller repair specific problems with the property or to request a seller credit to be given to the buyer at the close of escrow in lieu of said repairs.

### Contingency for Sale of Buyer's Property (COP)
A form that states the offer to buy a property is contingent upon the sale of the buyer's property. This form gives the buyer the right to back out of the contract if they are unable to sell their house within a specified period of time.

### Cancellation of Contract
A form that must be signed by both parties that cancels a signed offer agreement, returns the earnest money to the buyer, and allows the seller to find a new buyer.

Many agents use a transaction coordinator to understand and execute these forms as well as to ensure they are all correctly submitted, complied with, and received by the agreed-upon due dates. However, even if you use a TC, your ability to fill out and explain these forms to your clients is still part of your duties as a fiduciary representative of your clients.

# Comparative Market Analysis
Comparative Market Analysis (CMA) is data-driven tool that agents use to determine the value of a home in any given market. Agents most often use CMAs when setting the list price for a property. CMAs are made up of three parts: homes actively for sale (actives), homes currently under contract (pending), and homes that have already closed (sold).

Any real estate agent can run a CMA through the MLS, but the best interpret the CMA for their clients, helping them to understand what they can reasonably expect to receive for their property. Develop this skill and you will increase your clients' confidence and trust in you. Before running a CMA, you'll want to choose the categories your MLS will show you. I like to include the following fields:

- Address
- City
- Price

- Days on market (DOM)
- Lot square footage
- House square footage
- Bedrooms
- Bathrooms
- List price
- Sale price

The resulting CMA will show a list of active homes on top, pending homes beneath that, and sold homes at the bottom. Sold homes let you know what you can expect your property to appraise for. They also show how long homes in a specific price range are sitting on the market before they sell.

Pending homes are the most important metric. They let you know which properties have gone into contract and are the best indicator of what buyers are looking for in a given market. Pay special attention to the condition, size, location, and price of pending properties. For example, are the homes all staged? If so, hire a staging company to stay competitive. A small amount of research like this will tell you the condition and price with which you want to position your listing.

Active homes are your competition. They show you what options buyers have available. You don't want to be priced higher than your competition. If there are a large number of active homes on the market, you should price conservatively. If there are a small number of active homes on the market, you can be more aggressive.

When you first look at a CMA, notice the shape of it. You're hoping to see a pyramid, with a small number of active properties on top, followed by a larger number of pending properties in the middle, and an even larger number of sold properties on the bottom. This indicates a healthy seller's market, and you can feel confident your listing will get a lot of showings, be more likely to receive multiple offers, and sit on the market for fewer days. Conversely, you don't want to see a high number of properties actively for sale and a low number pending and sold. This means a small number of buyers will be competing over a large number of houses, which typically leads to properties sitting on the market for more days.

The second thing you should check is the DOM of the pending and sold listings. You are hoping for a lower number of days before a property goes into contract. In most markets, less than thirty days is a strong seller's market, thirty to sixty days is an average market, and more than sixty days is becoming a buyer's market. In some areas with less demand, the average DOM can be much higher.

The third thing to look at is the list-to-sell ratio. In a strong seller's market, homes will sell for more than the list price as they typically get multiple offers and buyers will have to complete to win the deal. Choose the fields "list price," "sale price," and "list-to-sell ratio" and have them all lined up in order. This way you can quickly see what each property was listed at, what it closed at, and what percentage of the sales price that it was. In cooler markets the list to sales price will be lower than 100 percent.

The fourth thing to look at is the DOM of the active listings. This shows how long your competition has been on the market. Your goal is to find the active listings that have been on the market the longest and do the opposite of what their agents have done. Look at the DOM for pending listings and establish that as a baseline for how long a house should sit on the market. If an active listing has a DOM higher than the baseline, that indicates there may be something wrong with the property and/or the agent did not market it correctly.

Some homes are priced too high. Others are in poor condition. By closely examining the features and pictures of each property, you can figure out why they are not selling for the price they are listed at. For example, some of the active listings will have small lots, poor decor/ upgrades, or too few bedrooms. You want to ensure that your listing is in better condition than the active homes that have not sold. If it isn't, you'll need to adjust your pricing to be lower than theirs.

The fifth thing to look at is whether the pending homes are selling for more than the sold homes. This is an indication that the market is improving and home prices are increasing. When this is the case, you should see a clear progression of rising prices from homes that sold six months ago all the way through to those that are actively for sale. Price per square foot is often the easiest metric to use for tracking this. Rising prices will often be accompanied by a decrease in DOM. If prices are not steadily rising, you cannot be as aggressive with your own listing.

The last thing to look for is pending properties that most closely match yours. When you find a close match, you've likely found a price point you can list your home at. If the market seems hot, you can adjust this price slightly higher. If it's cooling off, consider listing slightly lower.

Practicing running and interpreting CMAs is essential to becoming a top producer. Consider asking your friends and family for their address so you can practice running CMAs. Not only will this give you an opportunity to improve your skills, but you will actually surprise several people with how much their home is really worth. When you combine this with practicing your listing presentation on them, you may find this leads to a large number of phone calls from friends and family—or someone they know—about selling their house!

## CMA Summary

1. Running CMA means very little. The value to your client is in your ability to interpret that data.
2. Active homes are your competition. Don't price above them.
3. Pending homes are your best metric. Aim to replicate their condition and price.
4. Sold homes are what an appraiser will use to assign a value to a home.
5. Seller's markets have CMAs shaped like a pyramid, with a large base of sold homes and a narrow top of active homes.
6. Watching prices change from sold to pending to active will give you a good idea which way the market is trending. If prices are increasing, the market is getting hotter. If they're decreasing, the market is cooling off.
7. Higher prices correlate with lower DOM. If homes sit for a longer amount of time, prices will hold steady or decrease.
8. Practicing running CMAs and interpreting them for your friends and family will not only help you improve, it will plant seeds in their heads to call you when they are ready to sell or want to know what their houses are worth.

# Always Working/Never Working

While this is more of a concept than a fundamental skill, learning to strike this delicate balance is critical to becoming a top-producing agent. If you work too much, you will be burned out and lose business due to inadequate follow-up and a poor attitude with leads and clients. If you don't work enough, you will lose business due to poor lead generation. To maximize your revenue, you must master the art of always working without becoming burned out.

Beware of the following signs of burnout:

## Once Easy Tasks Are Now Difficult

Ever feel like your cellphone weighs five pounds and just looking at it hurts? That's burnout. When you are in a state of flow, experiencing momentum, and feeling refreshed, tasks like running CMAs, answering emails, and returning agents' calls are fun and exciting. You can see the dollar signs and can't wait to give great service. When you're burned out, every little thing you have to do feels difficult, and you need some time away from work.

## Chronic Fatigue

Feeling tired for no reason is another sign of burnout. This fatigue is often accompanied by insomnia. When you're mentally exhausted and your brain needs a break, you'll often experience this as physical exhaustion. Feeling tired or sluggish all the time and wanting daytime naps means you need to step away from work for a while.

## Inability to Concentrate

If your mind wanders when it should be focused, work becomes difficult and you are more likely to make mistakes. That's a sign of mental fatigue. When you catch yourself constantly daydreaming, forgetting what you were working on, or wanting to surf the web or mindlessly watch videos, you are experiencing burnout.

## Loss of Joy

Is there anything better than the feeling of getting a new listing? Walking away from an appointment with a signed listing agreement can transport you to cloud nine. When you're taking listings, putting clients into contract, and closing deals but still not feeling joyful, that is a big red flag. The pleasure we derive from being successful and helping clients motivates us and fuels our productivity. Without it we are vulnerable to making mistakes and giving poor service. Protect your joy. If you feel less than enthused about things that normally pump you up, give yourself some major downtime.

## Irritability

When your muscles are fatigued, they hurt and scream for a break. Your personality does the same, but manifests as irritability—especially over small things. If someone's tone is setting you on edge or you're ready to cuss them out because it takes them four rings to answer the phone, you may need some time off. As salespeople, our job is to remain positive when others are negative, confident when they are uncertain, and levelheaded when they are overly emotional. If you're getting irritated too easily, you can't do your job.

## Lack of Excitement over a New Lead

We work hard to find new leads, so getting one should be exciting. But if you're burned out, a new lead doesn't sound like more revenue; it just sounds like more work. If you find yourself apathetic or even annoyed about the prospect of converting a new lead, consider taking a vacation or at least a mental health day.

## Failure to Ask for Referrals

Not asking your SOI or clients for referrals is a sign you're afraid you might get a new lead—which is a sign of burnout. Asking for referrals should be as natural to you as walking or breathing. If it's not, that may be a sign you need some time off.

As a new agent I found myself constantly worrying about a lengthy list of things that would affect my business like my leads using a different Realtor, my offers not being accepted, or making a mistake in escrow. The accumulation of these fears led to quick and oppressing burnout. I really had no idea the impact they were having on my mental well-being, or even how important protecting my well-being was. As I've matured as an agent, I've recognized the emotional (and financial) cost of worrying about things I cannot control and being ruled by fear of failure.

Your personality, mindset, and response time are critical to your effectiveness as an agent. You won't do a good job representing clients or make them feel comfortable using you as their agent if you don't bring your A game to your interactions with them or, even worse, fail to follow up with confidence in a timely manner. Make your mental well-being a priority and you'll find it much easier to always be working!

Mastering the fundamentals will take you far in real estate sales. Practice them with your friends, family, acquaintances—anybody who will let you. As you become more confident and competent in applying these fundamentals, success will follow!

# ➡ KEY CHAPTER POINTS

- Every endeavor has fundamental skills that are crucially important to success. Committing to learning real estate fundamentals is non-negotiable.
- It may seem obvious, but your confidence will grow as you become comfortable learning the fundamentals. Stick through it and keep learning!
- Create a file and a cover sheet before you need to write an offer to shorten the time required to do so. It will help when you're in a pinch.
- Storing your client's files in the cloud will allow you or team members to access them from anywhere.
- Collect your clients' preapproval letter, proof of funds, and a template for a love letter ahead of time so you're not scrambling to put them together at the last minute.
- Building rapport with a listing agent will help you put your clients into contract.
- Practice running searches in the MLS before you have to do so for clients.
- Schedule drip campaigns to show your clients properties that match their criteria without having to conduct a manual search every day.
- Learning to choose the right homes to show your buyer clients will have a massive impact on how many homes you sell.
- Ask open-ended questions as well as pointed questions to ensure you are finding the right homes for your clients.
- Before showing a home, enter all relevant data in your phone's calendar so that it's readily accessible, which will save you time.
- Debrief your clients after each round of showings to stay in tune with how they are feeling and what they want.
- CMAs represent a snapshot of the market and are used to set the list price for a home. Your interpretation of the CMA is the value you provide to your clients. Do not run a CMA and send it to clients to figure out for themselves.
- Active listings are your competition, pending listings are your goal to match, and sold listings show you how the market is trending.

- DOM is an important metric and will help you determine how fast inventory is moving at any given time. The lower the DOM, the higher prices will trend.
- Working too much, which can lead to burnout, will actually cost you money. Learn to identify the signs of burnout, and make protecting your mental well-being a top priority.

## CHAPTER EIGHT

# MINDSET

When I was young, I was absolutely in love with the game of basketball. I fantasized about it, studied it, and practiced it. I desperately wanted to be as good a player as possible. But while my understanding of the game grew by leaps and bounds, my skills did not. Excellence in basketball, as with everything else in life, depends on two things: your knowledge and your ability to *apply* that knowledge. My vertical leap, speed, and size were all better than average but not nearly good enough to play professionally. I had the knowledge, but my physical limitations prevented me from applying it.

As a young man, this broke my heart. As a middle-aged man, I've come to see it as a blessing. Because I did not achieve what I wanted to with basketball, I became extremely motivated to seek success in other endeavors—like real estate. The biggest difference between real estate and basketball is that what determines your ability to apply your knowledge is not a physical characteristic but a mental one—that is, your mindset.

Just as your physical traits dictate your ceiling in sports, your mental traits will dictate how much success you're capable of achieving in sales. Those with a strong mindset—even if they have less experience, less knowledge, and less natural sales ability—will absolutely outperform those with a weaker mindset.

You have the power to become as successful as you want in real estate sales. Nobody can stand in your way except you, thanks to the influence of self-limiting beliefs. We all have them: pessimism, fear, complacency. Those are the things that contribute to a weak mindset and keep you from realizing your full potential. Attributes such as motivation, focus, confidence, and momentum, on the other hand, contribute to a strong mindset. And when it comes to being successful, nothing matters more than having a strong mindset.

This chapter will focus on how to develop these positive attributes so that, just like an Olympic athlete, you can perform at your highest possible level. Also like an elite athlete, you will inspire those around you to give their best and reach new levels of success.

## Motivation

The most important component of a powerful mindset is motivation. Motivation can refer to two things: the reasons we act in a certain way and our willingness to act. The first relates to our desire to do something; the second to how powerful that desire is. If you want to improve your motivation, you need to focus on both. What is it that drives you, and how powerfully are you driven? As we dig deeper into our own psyches, we find that the two are often related.

## Your Clients' Motivation

Unmotivated clients will, in essence, steal your time—but only if you let them. If you misinterpret your clients' motivation, does it really matter? Yes! Getting this wrong can amount to losing tens of thousands of dollars of commissions. The time you spend with clients—talking with them, looking up houses for them, showing them properties, updating them on the market—is time that is *not* going directly toward a paycheck unless they are truly motivated to buy or sell. Clients will almost always enjoy benefiting from your knowledge and expertise. It's up to you to be judicious about who you share that knowledge and expertise with if you want to run a profitable business.

It's important to keep in mind that your time, energy, and effort are finite resources: There's only so much of you to go around. Having the wisdom and discernment to choose which clients to invest in is essential to the top-producing agent's mindset. It can literally be the difference between generating revenue and going broke.

## Surrounding Yourself with Motivated Clients

In his book *Willpower Doesn't Work*, author Benjamin Hardy makes the case that our willpower is a temporary solution to our problems and fails us quite often. He says that surrounding ourselves in a healthy environment that challenges, rewards, and naturally encourages us to be more like people we admire is a much more efficient way to improve our lives and achieve the results we want. For the top-producing agents, this means surrounding yourself with clients who are motivated to close deals and who truly appreciate your services.

Because I *only* work with people who are very motivated to sell, I have a nearly 100 percent success rate in selling my clients' homes. Additionally, nearly all my buyer clients will write offers on the houses I show them. Why? Because I know my worth, and I won't give my valuable time, effort, and attention to anyone whose goals are not aligned with mine.

This makes my lead generation much more fun. I know that the effort I put into each client interaction is going to return to me in the form of financial compensation. I rarely expend effort that doesn't lead to revenue in some form. This keeps me motivated and loving my job. As long as you work only with motivated clients, you will protect your own motivation—and keeping your personal motivation level high is one of the pillars of maintaining the positive and productive mindset of a top producer. Consider the following script, which I use with every buyer client when I want to get a better feel for their motivation level.

**Me:** "Hey there, Josh. Thanks for taking my call today. I had a few questions I wanted to go over with you to make sure I do the best job possible when it comes to serving your interests."

**Client:** "Hey, no problem, David. What's up?"

**Me:** "Well, how would you describe your motivation level on a scale of one to ten?"

**Client:** "Hmmm, I guess I never really thought about it like that. Maybe a seven?"

**Me:** "Okay, great. And what does a seven mean to you?"

**Client**: "Well, I don't know. Like, I would buy a house if it was a great deal, but I don't *have* to buy anything. And I'm not going to feel pressured to move on something unless I know it's a great deal and stupid to pass up."

**Me:** "Okay, that's helpful. Imagine we look at fifteen homes, and you find several that would work for you but aren't so incredibly impressive that they scream, 'Buy me now!' Would that mean you'd pass them up?"

**Client:** "Well, it's hard to say. Until I see them, I really can't know. But yeah, I guess I probably wouldn't buy anything if that was the case. Why? Are you saying you don't want to work with me because I won't jump at just anything that pops up?"

**Me:** "Not at all. It's just important I understand where you're coming from, and these answers are exactly what I needed. I've done this with all different kinds of clients, and I've learned that some things can go terribly wrong if I don't ask these questions up front, ya know?"

**Client:** "Yeah, that makes sense."

**Me:** "Right, so I've found that the single most important thing I can do in this process is to make sure I match my motivation to yours. The reason I'm asking you about your motivation is because it wouldn't be fair to make you responsible for matching mine. You don't do this as often as I do, so I'd like to tailor my approach to match yours, instead of vice versa. Make sense?"

**Client:** "Yeah, I suppose that part does. But why does it matter? You work for me, right?"

**Me:** "In a sense, yes, of course. In another sense, no. I don't 'work' for you in that I'm not going to make you pay me. If you don't close on a house, I will consider that I did not do my job correctly, and it's not fair to ask you to compensate me if I fail. If I truly worked for you, you'd have to pay me just like in any other job. In another sense I *do* work for you—because I'll be working to represent your interests in this transaction. In order to do that, I need to know more about those interests."

**Client:** "Right, okay."

**Me:** "So, basically there are two ways, in my experience, that this can go wrong. I can be more motivated than you, or you can be more motivated than me. Both result in a bad experience for each of us. It's tricky but important that we get this right! If I am more motivated to help you buy a house than you are to buy one, I'll be working hard to find you deals, doing a lot of research to save you time, and making this a priority for me. I'll be sending you information and expecting a prompt response. If you're not as motivated as me, I will come across as pushy at best and greedy at worst. You won't like how it feels because I will come across as pressuring you. Surely you can see how that would be bad, right?"

**Client:** "Yes, I would not like that at all. I actually hate when agents do that."

**Me:** "Exactly. I'd feel horrible if that happened. But that's not the only way I can get this wrong. The other side of the coin is just as bad, if not worse. If I'm *not* as motivated as you, you'll be sending me houses you want me to look up, checking your email daily to see what work I've done, and expecting me to do research to save you time. When I'm not meeting those expectations, I will come across as lazy, disinterested, and not caring about your needs. That will be terrible for our relationship as well. Can you see that?"

**Client:** "Yeah, I suppose you're right. Okay, I think I know what you're getting at now."

**Me:** "Good! It's super important to me that I do a great job, and I can't do that unless our motivations match. I'm willing to adjust my motivation to meet yours. When I hear you tell me you're at a seven, that tells me you don't want me to be working very hard to find you a property; you kind of just want me to keep an eye out for that screaming deal that may come along every so often and notify you when it does. Is that okay with you?"

**Client:** "Oh, no, not at all! I definitely can't wait around to find a house. I'm just really scared about feeling pressured into buying the wrong house."

**Me:** "Okay, great, this is why I'm glad we had this conversation. What if we make a deal right now? I promise I will not pressure you to buy a house that I do not believe is the best option for you; but if I find one, I promise I *will* pressure you into buying it if it is. You promise that if we find a house that works better for you than your current situation, you'll buy it; and you promise that if I send you anything you don't think works, you'll be honest with me about your thoughts and feelings and not feel obligated to write an offer just to please me. Do you think we can commit to that?"

**Client:** "Yeah, that sounds great actually. I already feel a little better. Thanks for this, David.

This script works for me in several ways. It helps explain the importance of matching motivation, helps me to understand the client's actual motivation, and prepares them for the fact that they will be writing offers on properties I find that work for them. Use this script with any buyer client when you aren't sure how motivated they are and how much time you should be spending with them.

Here are some follow-up questions to help you better determine the expectations and motivation level of leads and clients:

- What will happen if we don't find you a home in the next month?
- What will happen if we don't get your home on the market in the next two months?
- What will prevent you from writing an offer on a home we find that you like?
- What are your biggest concerns with this process?
- What does a win look like to you?

- What are you looking for from me more than anything else?
- What are some experiences you've had with other real estate agents that you'd like to avoid in our relationship?
- I've found that there are four levels of motivation a buyer can have. Which one do you feel fits you best?
  - I need to find a house as soon as possible, and I will be buying one regardless.
  - I'd really like to find a home, but it has to be the right one. I'll write an offer immediately when I find it.
  - I might buy a house, but I don't need to. The house needs to motivate me, because I am not inherently motivated.
  - I will buy a screaming deal if it's convenient for me.

## Your Motivation

Understanding what motivates your clients is huge. Understanding what motivates *you* is even bigger. Most top-level businesspeople will tell you that the critical deciding factor in someone's success is their level of personal motivation. People are capable of incredible feats when they want something badly enough. They are also capable of squandering all their gifts and hiding from the harsh realities of the world. The same person who is capable of becoming a neurosurgeon can end up spending a lifetime eating junk food on the couch if they aren't motivated.

Entire libraries on motivation already exist, so I'm not going to delve too deeply here. But one thing I've learned about motivation is this: The goal is not "get" more of it but to remove the barriers blocking the motivation you already have. Are you afraid of success because you don't think you deserve it? Are you afraid of failure, so you never really try? Do you secretly think you're just not smart enough to be a top producer? If so, you're not alone. Most of us struggle with doubts like these, often without even realizing it.

If you dig deep enough, you'll find that the person holding you back is you. You do have motivation. It's just buried underneath something else that prevents you from feeling and experiencing it. The single most important thing you can do to improve your motivation is to determine your so-called Big Why. Understanding what truly matters to you and the reason behind it is key to unlocking your personal motivation.

How do you know whether lack of motivation is your problem? You're likely short on motivation if:

- You aren't already succeeding
- The thought of success is scary or intimidating to you
- You think negative thoughts when someone says, "You can do it!"
- You're not doing the work of lead generation
- Those who work for you are not excited about their role and future opportunities
- Your fears are louder than your dreams
- Your leads are not consistently moving down your sales funnel
- You're not excited about your next client or opportunity
- People can't hear excitement in your voice
- You're not looking for a way around a problem but are focusing on the enormity of the problem
- You aren't making meaningful progress every single day

If you want to be a successful agent, you must learn to harness the power of motivation and make it serve you. Here are some of the ways we fail to harness motivation, or even worse, push it away.

## Not Capitalizing on Momentum

Momentum has a huge impact on motivation. Finding yourself in a flow state, in which everything comes easily, often results from momentum. When you have momentum and everything seems easy, staying motivated is easier too. How can you capitalize on momentum? When you get a buyer into contract, share that story with other leads so they'll be more likely to go into contract themselves. When you negotiate a great deal for a seller, tell all their neighbors about it so they'll reach out to you when they want to sell. Don't waste your momentum. Use it to your advantage so you can stay motivated!

## Not Rewarding Yourself

When you achieve a victory, like selling a house or taking a new listing, you've got to make the most out of the positive feelings that result. Your brain has a natural reward system, and it will release dopamine, norepinephrine, and serotonin to make you feel really good about your achievement. If you're afraid to feel too good because you don't want to get too high and then fail, you'll subconsciously inhibit these chemicals from being released and prevent yourself from enjoying your victory. This robs you of the reward that your inner sense of motivation is chasing.

Go out to dinner to celebrate closings. Let your office staff cheer for you. Call your closest friends and let them build you up—they want to hear about your wins, and you'll enjoy their support when they congratulate you. Get acquainted with feeling good when you do the things you're supposed to—like making your daily calls or contacts. Enjoy the journey, and you'll find yourself setting bigger and bigger goals—and achieving them.

## Not Recharging

Burnout will kill motivation faster than anything else. Many people think they can work forever without taking a day off or going on vacation. I used to be one of them, but I learned this was a mistake. When you make it a priority to recharge your batteries, even if it means taking time away from work, you'll end up being more effective, productive, and successful.

Remember that you are not a machine but a human being. Part of being human is that we work in cycles: waking and sleeping, exercising and resting, working and playing. If we want to be successful on one side of the cycle, we need to spend time on the opposite end as well. A well-rested, well-balanced version of yourself will be much more motivated than a worn-out, miserable one. Your clients and leads can recognize which version of you they're encountering more than you think.

## Engaging in Negative Self-Talk

People who engage in negative self-talk are often unaware they do. Having a poor self-image is like seeing your reflection in a dirty mirror—you believe this is how you look and don't realize it's not how everyone else sees you. Negative self-talk prevents you from feeling bold, confident, and worthy. In fact, it kills motivation! If you do make progress that gets you excited and confident, negative self-talk douses your positive feelings before they can grow.

The best way to overcome this is to get real with yourself about the fact that it's going on, then turn to people you know and trust and ask for their objective opinion of you. Doing that takes faith—not to mention—courage. It may not be easy, but it's important. If you want to stay motivated, you must silence your inner critic by getting clear on your strengths and focusing on the unique value you bring to your clients as you go about your work.

## Not Breaking Goals into Bite-Sized Chunks

It's easy to get overwhelmed by the enormity and complexity of huge goals. To overcome this, break them down into smaller ones. In an article on Inc.com,[7] former Navy SEAL Andy Stumpf and host of the podcast, *Cleared Hot*, shared how he survived BUD/S (Basic Underwater Demolition/SEAL) training. This training is considered one of the toughest rites of passage out there, and few complete it successfully. Andy says the secret to overcoming the rigorous physical and mental challenges is to start thinking small:

> There's two ways you can look at BUD/S. It's 180 days long. Or you can look at it as a sunrise and a sunset, 180 times. ...The advice I was given was, 'Don't look at Hell Week as a five-day pipeline. Just make it to your next meal, because they have to feed you every six hours.' So if I can stack six hours on six hours on six hours, and just focus on getting to the next meal...it doesn't matter how much I'm in pain, doesn't matter how cold I am...if I can just get to the next meal, get a mental reprieve and mental reset...then I can go on.

In other words, those who can focus on what is right in front of them and devote all their resources to that are much more likely to be successful than those who are overwhelmed by the task as a whole and its seemingly impossible requirements.

Instead of focusing on selling one hundred homes a year, focus on making twenty contacts a day. You don't need to think about all twenty conversations at once. You just need to concentrate on the one you are having now. You don't need to convince someone to sell their home. You just need to win them over so that when they are ready to sell, they choose you to represent them. Learning to focus on the small tasks instead of the big goal can keep your motivation and confidence level high, regardless of the situation you're in.

---

**7** Jeff Haden, "Why Thinking Small Is Your Best Defense in Tough Situations," April 1, 2020, accessed at https://www.inc.com/jeff-haden/feel-overwhelmed-overworked-out-of-answers-a-navy-seal-says-1-literally-small-decision-separates-successful-people-from-all-rest.html.

### Not Setting Reasonable Milestones

To succeed at focusing small, keep your expectations reasonable and your bite-sized chunks achievable. Not only will your mind tackle each smaller goal more effectively, but your motivation will get a natural boost as you reach each milestone along the way to achieving your ultimate goal. We respond well to perceived progress; setting unreasonable milestones for yourself will rob you of that satisfaction.

### Not Writing Down Your Goals

When we write down our goals and look at them frequently, we train our brain's reticular activating system (RAS) to recognize opportunities and call them to our attention more often. If you want to be successful, you've got to get your subconscious working for you, not against you. Writing down your goals will remind you of your priorities and keep you moving forward toward achieving them. And—yes, you guessed it—perceived progress increases motivation.

### Not Tracking Your Progress

If you aren't keeping track of the progress you're making, you can't enjoy making it! Productivity coaches know this, and that's why they insist their clients track their progress. There's a big difference between making as many phone calls as you can and simply trusting that you made at least twenty versus writing down the name of each person you talk to and checking a box that says, "I talked to twenty people today."

The first method will get the contacts made but leave you without satisfaction. The second will give you a sense of accomplishment. When you're feeling good about yourself, it's that much easier to make the next day's calls. Why rob yourself of this positive reinforcement? Keep daily records of your small goals and continue achieving them to keep yourself motivated.

### Expecting Perfection

When we set excessively high standards for ourselves, we face massive anxiety every time we have to undertake a new task. That's because the fear of failure weighs on our subconscious. The result? Waning motivation that takes the form of procrastination.

The problem with procrastination is that it gets worse the longer it goes on. If it was hard to start that big undertaking yesterday, it will be even more difficult today, when you're one day further behind. Tomorrow will be even worse. To avoid this vicious cycle, start with lowering your expectations of yourself. Perfection is the enemy of progress. It stops you from building momentum, prevents you from hitting small milestones, and robs you of the joy hitting those milestones.

Your mind is designed to work a certain way, looking for natural rewards and releases to keep it motivated and hungry for better results. It's not wired for perfection, and your subconscious knows that you are not perfect and never will be. This creates an uphill climb for perfectionists, who think their high standards will prevent them from making mistakes. In fact, those high standards actually prevent them from making progress. Be kind to yourself and learn to take joy in becoming better, *not* completely perfect.

## Focus

The ability to remain focused is the second pillar of a healthy mindset. Because of the incremental nature of the real estate sales process, most of your efforts will be directed toward achieving many small victories that culminate in the ultimate success of a sale. If you lose focus along the way, you can lose all the progress you've already accomplished. It's easy to charge out of the gate full of energy and motivation. What's difficult is to sustain that energy and motivation day in and day out. The ability to maintain focus is essential to becoming a top-producing agent.

With so many tasks competing for a real estate agent's attention each day, one of the biggest threats we face is spending large amounts of time and energy on work that doesn't actually make money. The "busywork" siren is seductive and appealing! When you know that what you should be doing is risking rejection by making phone calls to ask for business, spending a few hours creating a marketing flyer can seem like an attractive alternative. Avoiding such traps is a crucial part of a top producer's work ethic.

In order to maintain focus, many productivity coaches recommend tracking key performance indicators (KPIs), which are the activities that will lead to success in a particular role. Committing to tracking these KPIs will lead to a successful business as they directly contribute to revenue. The following table illustrates the difference between activities that lead directly to revenue and those that can be justified as necessary but ultimately rob you of time and don't earn money:

| KPI | PRODUCTIVITY KILLER |
| --- | --- |
| Setting listing or buyer appointments | Looking up houses on the MLS for non-preapproved, unmotivated leads |
| Delivering listing or buying presentations | Editing the video you made for social media until it looks perfect |
| Having conversations about real estate in which you ask for business | Handing out business cards at the end of a conversation in which you did not make your intentions clear |
| Asking your SOI if they know of anyone looking to buy or sell | Attending a happy hour to listen to the stories of other real estate agents and calling it "networking" |
| Farming a neighborhood | Spending too much time designing your own logo |
| Attending events and talking about real estate while you meet new people and gather their contact information | Spending too much time creating your own website |
| Calling past clients to check in and ask for business | Researching current market data/trends and never talking with anyone about it |

There are so many things an agent can do as part of a day's work. But the best have learned that only a small number of those things result in new clients and revenue, and they devote most of their time to those activities.

This concept is embodied in the so-called Pareto Principle, named after the Italian economist Vilfredo Pareto. Also known as the 80/20 Rule, it states that 80 percent of consequences stem from 20 percent of causes. This rings true for real estate, where about 80 percent of business is generated by just the top 20 percent of agents. Success is not evenly distributed!

The Pareto Principle suggests that we must remain focused on the 20 percent of activities that will result in 80 percent of our revenue. Top-producing agents have mastered this. In order to avoid distractions, consider the following list that shows the many activities you can conduct in a day that do *not* lead to new business or revenue yet can be justified as important work.

| | |
|---|---|
| Attending signings | Showing homes |
| Attending photo sessions for your listings | Scheduling inspections |
| Attending inspections | Running CMAs |
| Creating a tagline | Putting on lockboxes |
| Researching different brokers | Creating marketing flyers |
| Answering every email to create inbox zero | Studying real estate "disruptors" |
| Writing all your own offers | Going on broker tours |
| Posting on social media when you don't get engagement | Creating vision boards |
| Paying for expensive ads to keep picky sellers happy | Doing your own transaction coordination |
| Making small talk with office staff or other Realtors | Scheduling open houses |

Now, I'm not saying these things do not need to get done—I am only saying that doing them will not get you paid. It's entirely possible to have someone else handle these items, perhaps even more effectively than you would. And that frees you up to focus on activities that will generate income. The following tools will help you avoid distractions and maintain your focus on the 20 percent of your activities that matter most.

## Calendars

Using a calendar to time block the most important tasks of your day will help you remain focused. As an agent, you usually won't have a boss dictating how to spend your time. Unfortunately, many of us languish under that kind of freedom. Instead, make your calendar your boss by strictly adhering to the time you block for important tasks like lead generation and other KPIs that will earn you revenue.

When engaging in time-blocked activities, do your best to guard against distractions. Stay focused by physically placing your phone (most agents' biggest distraction) across the room from you. You can also commit to avoiding social media and turn off notifications.

## Coaching

Hiring a professional coach can offer a huge ROI for your time and money. A good coach can help shorten your learning curve, inspire you to reach for goals you never thought possible, and keep you motivated and excited while doing it. Most of us learn from mistakes and coaches help us to achieve success more quickly.

When choosing a coach, look for someone who:
- understands your strengths and talents;
- understands your weaknesses and liabilities;
- has accomplished, or knows how to accomplish, what you want to do;
- communicates in a way you understand;
- is committed to making you uncomfortable for your ultimate good; and
- has values similar to yours.

In my own sales career, I've hired a real estate coach; a mindset coach to help me stay focused, energized, and at my best; and a performance psychologist to help me remove the mental and emotional barriers that can sometimes prevent me from achieving my own potential. Investing in coaching is an excellent way to develop and maintain focus, and a good coach is worth their weight in gold.

## Accountability

Accountability is important for success in any venture. Most of us take it for granted, because it's usually other people—parents, teachers, coaches, bosses—who hold us accountable.

When you become a real estate agent, unless you join a team with built-in accountability, you will quickly find that you must supply it yourself. Desiring accountability is about as sexy as desiring vegetables. None of us want it but we all need it. If you take your success seriously, you will take accountability seriously as well! Consider the following story from two of my real estate mentors—David Osborn (co-author of *Bidding to Buy* and author of *Wealth Can't Wait*) and Pat Hiban (creator and host of the podcast *Real Estate Rockstars* and author of *6 Steps to 7 Figures*.)

In 1997 David and Pat met at a conference they were attending to learn new ways to improve their businesses and personal lives. They soon realized they were both fiercely committed to becoming more successful, and a friendship was born. As David and Pat looked for better ways to serve each other, they realized that accountability was more important than anything else when it came to providing true friendship.

Pat, generally a happy, charismatic guy, was nonetheless ruthless with David about making sure he achieved his goals. This brought out David's competitive nature and he developed great respect for Pat in the process. True to the law of reciprocity, David then began holding Pat just as accountable as Pat had been holding him, and their friendship deepened. Eventually, they met my first real estate mentor, Tim Rhode, who wound up collaborating with them on the book, *Tribe of Millionaires* (along with Mike McCarthy).

Ask David or Pat why they became such close friends, and they'll both say it was their mutual accountability. These men, real estate connoisseurs at heart, both understood just how important accountability was to becoming their very best—and they made it the foundation of their friendship.

If you aren't achieving your goals despite extensive training and knowledge, you could be suffering from a lack of accountability. Whether you find it with a friend, coworker, coach, or by joining an accountability group, make a concerted effort to bring accountability into your business. In fact, just signing up for a Premium membership on BiggerPockets. com should boost your accountability. Your focus will naturally improve once you have to account to someone for how you are actually spending your time.

## Confidence

Confidence can be tricky to describe, but we know it when we feel it. It becomes especially powerful, and important, when you find yourself in an environment filled with uncertainty. Confidence can be a luxury when you are relatively safe, but it is a necessity when you are facing risk and lack a clear path forward.

In 2006, I entered the police academy in Pittsburg, California, and began my law enforcement career. The first thing I learned is that the very idea that you are "trained to know what to do" in chaotic or dangerous situations is ridiculous. Nobody can know what to do, with any kind of consistency, in emergencies since they are rare by definition. And yet one of my primary roles as a police officer was to solve problems in emergencies, something I had to do numerous times over the course of my career.

Many people who have repeatedly dealt with uncertainty arrive at a place, emotionally and intellectually, that frees them from excessive worry. They've made peace with the fact that there's not always a clear-cut right thing to do but that some decisions are better than others. They've come to feel comfortable in their ability to make sound—not perfect—decisions in the face of more variables than they can control or even be aware of. That is how I describe confidence.

People who lack confidence will hesitate. It's natural to freeze in place when you're unsure of the right thing to do and feel you have to evaluate every possible consequence of every possible action you might take. If this describes you, as an agent when faced with decision-making in the rapidly changing and emotionally charged situations that arise during transactions, your indecisiveness will leave your clients experiencing anxiety and fear. To be a top real estate agent, you *must* be able to inspire confidence in your clients. When you do, your clients will take your advice and let you guide them through the transaction. But in order to inspire confidence in others, you must feel confident yourself.

In real estate sales, you won't know exactly what to do most of the time. There are so many paths you can take, and each of those paths will have risks and rewards, pros and cons. Each will have a best-case scenario in which your client wins and a worst-case scenario in which they lose. That is the reality of negotiation. That is the reality of a real estate transaction with two professional agents trying to navigate the murky waters of two sets of clients' volatile emotions. This is what you signed up for!

I'm able to take action despite my fears because of the confidence I've developed in making quick decisions, practicing my skills, and understanding the game I'm playing. You can learn to do the same. How do you go about building this inner confidence? First, you must accept that you cannot control your results, but you *can* control the actions you take and the amount of effort you put into those actions. Focusing on actions instead of results is the first mental shift you must make in order to begin building confidence.

As a basketball player, I used to hate missing shots. As the ball left my hands, I would try to "will" it into the basket. Eventually, I came to accept that once the ball left my hands, what happened next was beyond my control. I could only control every action I took leading up to that moment, such as how hard and how often I practiced. Accepting this opened me up to a freedom I hadn't felt before. I learned that I could hold myself responsible only for the actions I took *before* the ball left my hands. When I stopped focusing on what I could not control (whether the ball went in or not), I naturally started to focus more on what was within my control (the effort I put into developing my skills).

When I began applying this approach to my real estate career, my conversion rates increased along with my confidence. By shifting focus from results to effort and practice, you'll achieve more of the results you desire! The following table shows several practical ways you can apply this concept as a real estate agent.

| THINGS YOU CAN PRACTICE AND IMPROVE | THINGS YOU CANNOT CONTROL |
| --- | --- |
| The content and delivery of your listing presentation | Whether or not the client chooses to list their house with you |
| Your creativity in developing solutions for problems in escrow | Whether or not things go wrong in escrow |
| Your skill in delivering proven scripts | How clients will respond to your offer to represent them |
| Your mastery of handling objections | Which objection the client will throw at you |
| The effort you put into protecting the client from negative emotions | How your client handles negative emotions, and who they blame them on |
| The number of contacts you make in a day | How many people have a house they want to buy or sell |
| The number of training classes you take | The quality of the instructors |
| The tenacity and speed with which you pursue leads | How loyal the lead is to you |
| The quality of questions you ask, and your skill in using questions to guide behavior | How motivated your lead is |

| THINGS YOU CAN PRACTICE AND IMPROVE | THINGS YOU CANNOT CONTROL |
| --- | --- |
| The breadth of your local market knowledge | How much your client values experience in an agent |
| How hard you work to protect your client's money | How much your client appreciates what you've done for them |
| The enthusiasm in your requests for business | The personalities and preferences of those you talk to |
| The level of genuine care and concern you have for those in your database | The quality of the character of those you talk to |

When you focus on results (such as how many houses you close in a month), you can easily become discouraged. When you focus on effort (such as how many contacts you made that month), you can stay encouraged and excited. The more you focus on developing your skills at income-generating activities, the sharper those skills will become. The sharper your skills, the more confidence you'll have and the easier it will be to achieve the big results we're all after.

Start with this small adjustment in your thinking: Focus on what you can control. As you direct your attention and effort to the fundamentals, you'll build confidence that will only grow over time.

## The Story of the Lumberjack

Larry Lumberjack traveled west to make it big in the lumber business. He paid the fees to get his license and bought an ax, boots, flannel shirts, and beard oil. Larry did some research on how to chop down a tree, watching YouTube videos and reading every book he could find on the topic. When he finally received his lumberjack license, he ventured into the forest to give it a go.

Larry learned his first lesson in timber harvesting pretty quickly— namely, that just because he was in a forest didn't mean there were a lot of trees. Larry had assumed that when he arrived, there would be plenty of opportunities to try out his hand, but as he wandered the land, he found it looked more like desert than forest. Nevertheless, Larry kept searching until he found his first small grove of pine trees. A lead, at least!

As Larry approached the trees, he began counting the money he would make from selling the wood and began to feel rich before he'd even broken a sweat. Full of excitement, Larry ran right at the first tree he saw and—*whap!*—delivered his first swing. The ax head missed the tree completely, struck a stone on the ground, and got chipped. Despite a blow to his confidence, Larry gathered himself up, took three more swings, and, unable to strike the tree squarely, had nothing to show for his effort. Tired, discouraged, and blaming the tree, Larry pulled himself together and moved on to a slightly smaller, slightly softer-looking maple.

Larry took a well-measured swing at the maple and finally had a solid cut! But with the ax head now buried in the tree trunk, Larry found himself with a new dilemma: How would he get it out? Several hours of effort later, Larry finally yanked the ax free and sat down to rest. Once he'd recovered, he felt a new wave of optimism and got back to work on the maple. Larry swung several times, but not once did he manage to hit the same spot as he had with his first swing. With a now-dull ax and worn-out muscles, Larry decided to call it a day.

The next morning, Larry woke up with a plan to look for a different tree that was readier to fall. After a few hours of searching, he found a skinny, tall tree. Larry believed he could knock it down with one solid swing. On his first swing, he hit the trunk dead center: a solid, respectable strike. But to Larry's surprise, the tree did not fall! He spent the rest of the day striking again and again at the same tree. Finally, Larry had to acknowledge that although he had done plenty of damage to the tree, he had not affected it structurally in any way. Devoid of confidence, he once again decided to call it a day.

The following morning, Larry woke up with a new plan: He would make up for his lack of experience by overcompensating with physical effort. Larry put everything he had into each blow, swinging as often and as fast as he could. After several hours, he noticed an increasingly strong pain in his hands. To his horror, he saw that huge, red blisters had begun to form. They slowly swelled to the point where he could no longer make a fist or grip his ax. Larry was overcome with humiliation as he realized the folly of his ways. Why had he believed he could go from zero to hero with no real training? Dejected and beaten down, Larry yet again called it a day.

That night, Larry dreamed that he was in a great wooded glen teeming with wildlife and more trees than he could imagine. In the distance he saw a tall, well-built figure carrying a large ax and standing next to a blue ox. It was the great Paul Bunyan himself! Bunyan was swinging his mighty ax with a force and skill unlike anything Larry had ever seen.

Larry marveled at how Bunyan knocked down all kinds of trees with equal ease. How did Bunyan make it look so simple? With a hearty laugh and a huge smile, Bunyan turned around to address Larry. The great lumberjack asked how he had fared that day. Larry told the truth: Not only had he not dropped a single tree, but he had ruined his ax, his hands, and his confidence. As Larry hung his head in shame, a laugh erupted that shook the entire forest.

"So, you don't know where the trees grow, you never practiced with an ax before your first day, and you didn't bother to sharpen it before you began, but you're worried you don't have what it takes to be a lumberjack?" the giant exclaimed. "Just what were you expecting—the trees to give up and fall down on their own?" Bunyan again rocked and roared with laughter. As tears welled up in his eyes, Larry replied, "I get it. But no one told me what to expect. I didn't know." The tears flowed freely as Larry realized how much disappointment and shame he had been holding in.

Seeming to peer directly into his Larry's soul, Bunyan said, "Wanting to make it big as a lumberjack is a worthwhile goal. But know that the trees will resist you, the groves will be hard to find, and the skill it takes to fell the trees cannot be bought or traded for. You have to look deep within yourself and remove any hurdles to mastery you find. A lumberjack must be equal parts strong and wise, skillful and smart. This is not a job; it's a lifestyle." Larry absorbed Bunyan's words. What a fool he had been to think he could just show up and strike it rich without practicing first!

Bunyan continued: "There is an art to this. No one, not even I, a great giant of a man, can swing an ax all day. If you want to spare your muscles, you must sharpen your ax. If you want to keep your ax sharp, you must commit to the work it takes to do so. If you want to be productive, you must choose wisely—not only your trees but how you approach striking them. Before you begin striking, look at them carefully and devise your best plan of attack." Just as Larry began to open his mouth to ask more questions, he woke from his slumber.

Larry lay there thinking. Now he could see that he had gone about things all wrong. Hard work was absolutely necessary, but it was no substitute for smart, skilled effort. Only by combining strength with experience, commitment, knowledge, wisdom, and a sharp ax could Larry succeed as a lumberjack. As he closed his eyes and drifted back to sleep, he vowed that tomorrow he would take on the task of learning to be a lumberjack, not just wildly trying to chop down trees.

Larry's story is similar to that of many new agents. With no idea what to expect, they walk into the unfamiliar world of real estate and have their confidence completely destroyed before they truly get started. Comparing themselves with experienced lumberjacks who choose their trees (or clients) more wisely, these new agents reach the premature conclusion that they are simply not meant for the business and quit before they ever really give themselves a chance.

If you haven't learned the fundamentals of the business, you have absolutely quit too soon. My advice to new agents is not to focus on metrics beyond your control, like how many listings you take and how many buyers you are working with. Instead, focus on the metrics you *can* control, like how many conversations you have with leads and how skilled you are at handling objections from skeptical clients.

Confidence is the result of repetitive action and proven competence. Sustained attention to detail in the fundamentals of your craft will yield a sharp ax, a body capable of sustained effort, and a trained eye for spotting the right trees. When we look at Larry Lumberjack's story, we can pull from it ten key lessons that top producers have all learned:

## 1. Focusing on results can be discouraging.

If you focus on how many trees you cut down before you've learned the basics of how to do your job, you're sure to be disappointed. This is especially true when you compare yourself with more established agents. Instead, focus on metrics that show growth and improvement and that empower you to achieve the results you want. Forcing yourself to have a large number of conversations about real estate will help you get over any awkwardness as early as possible, and you'll feel more comfortable discussing it with clients. This leads to a sharp lead-generation ax.

The same holds true for other fundamentals, like delivering buyer and listing presentations, running CMAs, answering common objections, and even filling out offer forms. When you are not confident in your ability to use the basic tools of your profession, it shows. As you grow in confidence with these tools, you will find yourself both feeling and acting more confident, and people will perceive you that way.

## 2. Discouragement can kill the desire to work.

When you become discouraged and lose confidence, even small tasks can seem overwhelming. Anxiety can make mountains out of molehills. Avoid this by keeping your goals small and your milestones reasonable to build confidence and limit discouragement.

## 3. Too much work creates blisters that ultimately slow you down.

You can't sustain a successful career through effort alone. Pure hard work is no substitute for skill; and if you rely on it more than you should, blisters will form that slow you down. Make sure you take time to recharge and rest, and develop a healthy rhythm throughout the day. If you succumb to burnout, you'll need a significant amount of time to recover, and your overall production will suffer.

## 4. The numbers game is for amateurs. Strategic skill is for top producers.

As a new agent, you'll often hear that it's all a numbers game. While there's some truth to that (you do want to track your KPIs), don't fall prey to the belief that pure volume is an excuse to avoid improving your skills. The "numbers game" philosophy is often a justification for brokers to skimp on providing training and shift the responsibility for developing your skills from themselves to you. Track your numbers but sharpen your fundamentals while doing so.

## 5. More swings equal more productivity.

While you don't want to burn out by swinging your ax too often, don't think that means the number of swings doesn't matter. It does! The more contacts you make in a day, the more opportunities you give yourself to be successful. When you connect with a lead, *make sure you continually chip away at that lead until they sign up to work with you.* When you do get a lead to sign up, don't stop "swinging away" at other leads. The amount of lead generation you do is the single most important metric to earning income as a real estate agent.

## 6. A sharper ax leads to more productivity.

If your ax connects with a lead but it's not sharp, you get less return for your effort. This is why sharpening your ax is so important. Learning what's going on in your market, how loans work, what the newest laws are, and how to help save your clients money are all powerful ways to sharpen the ax of your skills and make significantly more progress with each contact. The sharper your ax, the less effort it takes to fell trees, and the more you can knock down with the same effort.

### 7. Top producers combine both effort and a sharp ax.

Effort and skill are like the two blades of a pair of scissors. When they work in tandem, you are most effective. Top producers don't focus on one blade over the other. They let their effort gain them experience, which sharpens their skills, which increases their confidence, which motivates them to work harder. This is the virtuous cycle that leads to big revenue.

### 8. Not all trees have the same worth.

Not all clients are motivated to the same degree, and not all deals will pay you the same amount of money. It requires wisdom, discernment, and skill to choose the most profitable objects of your effort. Some trees will require so much work they aren't worth the trouble, while others may go down easily if you apply a small amount of concentrated, urgent effort. Learn what a good client and a good deal look like, and train yourself to chase them more vigorously than those of less value to you.

### 9. Chopping a tree without bringing it all the way down is a waste of effort.

Larry could have chopped an entire forest full of trees 90 percent of the way down and still wound up not only penniless but also exhausted and discouraged to boot. Build your confidence by ensuring that your efforts come all the way to fruition. When someone is in your funnel, commit to guiding them all the way down, and don't get discouraged when you experience setbacks along the way. Ten clients who stop progressing when they're halfway down the funnel are worth the same as zero clients in the funnel to start with—and you'll never get back all the time and energy you invested in them.

### 10. As your career progresses, you'll be able to chop down different types of trees.

When you first start, you'll go after any tree you can find. Beggars can't be choosers! As your skill level increases, you'll become much pickier about when to swing your ax and what types of trees to chop down. The quality of the leads and clients you pursue will improve as your career progresses. This is a great confidence booster.

In addition to selling better houses, working less frequently with buyers, and raising your price point, you'll also be doing lead generation to find employees, assistants, interns, or agents. The principles in this book, and the nature of the funnel, will not change—but your targets will!

# CHAPTER ▶ NINE

# APPLICATION

A successful career in real estate sales is a multifaceted endeavor. Your success will depend partly on your understanding of the tasks necessary to be a real estate agent. As a new agent, learning "what to do" will often dominate your time.

True success in real estate sales is *how* you do your job. The way you explain things to your clients and carry yourself throughout your day will have a bigger impact on the amount of business you end up with than your knowledge of the mechanics of the job. These are underappreciated, if not neglected, aspects of real estate sales. Too many agents don't understand that the way they present themselves to others is the single biggest influence on the way people respond to them. The *how* is even more important than the *what*.

While the knowledge you seek as a new agent may seem incredibly valuable, to those you are trying to win over, it's almost insignificant. Most of those you are trying to attract as clients don't understand the job of a real estate agent and may not even know what separates a good agent from a bad one. All they know is how you make them feel.

## The Four C's

Getting started in any new endeavor is always a challenge. The more prestigious or difficult the endeavor, the greater the challenge. I learned this lesson in the police academy. We started off with sixty-four recruits and ended up with forty-eight. The length and difficulty of the process, as well as the focus required to complete it, separated those who were suited for a career in law enforcement from those who were not.

I noticed that those who did best embraced the level of commitment required and enlisted their loved ones to help them stick to it. These recruits explained to their family that they would need their support—whether with running errands, making meals, or helping them study for tests. I learned the importance of getting buy-in from those around me and making clear to them what they could expect from me.

I also observed that the recruits who could endure the pain and discomfort best were those who responded well to the training and therefore developed the skills necessary to succeed in the challenging world of law enforcement. Those who could not push through their initial discomfort never gave themselves the chance to develop those essential skills, and quit before they could develop the capability to do the job they had signed up for.

Finally, I realized that the learning never stopped. Once we successfully completed our training in the highly structured, militaristic world of the academy, we were thrust into environments that were almost the complete opposite: the streets and the jails. This forced us to transition from having to do everything we were told to having to figure most things out on our own, without incurring the disappointment of experienced officers or the criticism of our supervisors.

I believe the main reason I became my office's top agent in my first year was because of the lessons I learned in the police academy and my ability to apply them in my new career. I want to pass those lessons, which I call the Four C's, on to you to help with your career transition.

## 1. Commitment

There is a big difference between the mindset, "I will commit to doing whatever it takes to succeed, no matter what" and the mindset of "Let me give it a try and see if I like it." The more worthwhile the endeavor, the less you will enjoy the process of getting started in it. If you want to succeed in the highly competitive, unstructured, and easy-to-get-lost-in world of real estate sales, you *must* have a "whatever it takes" mentality.

Every top-producing agent shares a commitment to doing, learning, or changing whatever is necessary in order to succeed. This mindset produces a humility that makes learning easier as well as a resilience that allows you to learn from mistakes. For example, if you commit to lead generation every day, eventually, you will get better at it. If you quit because you don't "like" it, you'll probably never get good at it.

## 2. Courage

As an agent, you will constantly be dealing with leads who reject you covertly. You will be giving your very best only to be told time after time you are not good enough. When you finally achieve a measure of success and get a client, you'll step right back out there to eat that rejection sandwich over and over again. If you are getting every listing you interview for, you aren't pursuing enough listings. If you never get told no, you aren't talking to enough people.

It takes courage to succeed in real estate sales—a lot. In order to have courage, you must also be fearful. In fact, courage could be described as facing down fear and taking action anyway. The more courage you have, the more successful you'll be. How can you take courageous action if you're avoiding fear? As contrary as it may sound, you must actually welcome, accept, and pursue fear if you want to grow and be successful in this business. Telling someone directly "I want to be your agent" is incredibly scary the first time you do it. Now I consider it a wasted conversation if I don't say that.

In fact, I was actually terrified to host open houses when first I started out. My assistant had to meet the lead at the front door, introduce herself, then bring them back to introduce them to me. Without her helping me face my fear of sales, strangers, and small talk, I never would have made it. Beyond fear lies the growth you've been aiming for. Finding others to take that journey with you (like Krista Keller, my assistant, did for me) will help you take courageous action earlier and more often.

## 3. Capability

If you want to become successful in a new or unfamiliar world, you've got to be able to adapt. If you aren't willing to take on whatever challenge comes, no matter how difficult it may feel, you cannot adapt and grow. The attitude you choose when it comes to looking at the problems you're facing will lead you to success or not—ultimately, this determines how capable you can be in any situation.

Real estate sales is a commission-based, dog-eat-dog world where those you're hoping to learn from are the same people you're competing against. There is so much to learn, and there are so few people who will care whether you succeed. Most agents think there are too many agents in the industry already. If you don't make it, nobody is going to be upset.

Your job is to show up, with courage, for your clients—be capable. Even when you're unsure of the best move to make or what to do, you *have* to be the voice of reason, the calming presence, and the cool head. Your clients are looking to you to ease their fears, and you want them to see a capable, courageous person when they see you.

## 4. Capacity

As soon as I graduated from the academy, I was thrown into a new environment: a high-security detention facility. Once I put in my time there, I moved on to marine patrol. After that came street patrol. Every new iteration of my career brought its own set of challenges and obstacles to adapt to and overcome. I had to learn how to handle new challenges and reach new and surprising levels of "success" in each role—therefore increasing my capacity each time.

In fact, I had to start the Four C's all over again in each new cycle.

1. Commit to the process of becoming great in a new role.
2. Courageously tackle the things that scared me and actively seek those things out.
3. Capably handle the requirements of the job and make sure everyone around me was aware of my ability to do the job well.
4. Increase my capacity to handle new challenges and difficulties—and reach new levels of achievement.

The Four C's can provide focus and encouragement when you feel lost and can't find your way forward.

# Expectations

If you look at the top-producing agents in your office, you will find they share a certain work ethic. They run their business like a business. They take their clients, their work, and their results seriously. They maintain consistent schedules and give their best all day, every day.

Conversely, struggling agents tend to have the most inconsistent schedules and lowest degree of commitment. In fact, real estate has a terrible reputation for agents not taking the career seriously. Ask most agents why they got into the business, and they'll tell you they were looking forward to working whenever they wanted to and not having to answer to a boss. The reality is that even though you will have flexible hours, you may work more than at other jobs; you will often work when your clients want you to, not when you want to; and not having a boss to hold you accountable may have a negative impact on your earnings.

In fact, when you get into real estate sales, you trade one boss for many. In this industry, our clients are our bosses, and if you want to be a top-producing agent, you'll want to have as many bosses as possible. Take a moment to consider what many believe to be one of the most sought after "dream jobs," a medical doctor—specifically a surgeon—in America. Compare that with becoming a real estate agent. In general, most doctors will attend four years of undergraduate school, four years of medical school, and three to seven years of residency. According to NerdWallet, the average medical student graduates with approximately $200,000 in debt. And according to Business Insider, the average surgeon's salary is approximately $255,000 a year. That means in order to get that "dream job" as a doctor, someone has to invest about $200,000 and prepare for eleven to fifteen years before starting full-time, unsupervised career work.

Let's compare that with the potential for an agent to make good money in sales versus the time required to get there. If we double the numbers from Chapter One and sell two listings a month and close two buyers a month, we will gross $330,000 in commissions. Even if our expenses doubled from selling one listing a month and one buyer a month to the tune of $100,000, that would still leave us with a profit of $230,000 a year.

Let's compare these two scenarios:

| COMPARISON | SURGEON | TOP-PRODUCING AGENT |
|---|---|---|
| Yearly Pay | $205,000 | $230,000 |
| Debt | $220,000 | Less than $1,000* |
| Time to acquire license before revenue can be made | 11–15 years | 3–6 months |
| Ability to leverage job | No | Yes |
| Lifestyle freedom | Very limited | Less limited |
| Ability to work remotely | No | Yes |
| Lifestyle tax write-offs | Very limited | Yes |
| Effort required to obtain license | Extremely high | Comparatively minimal |

**\*** The cost of getting a real estate license in California is typically $400–1000.

If I told you that you as a real estate agent you could make more money than a doctor, start making it eleven to fifteen years sooner, and incur little to no debt in the process, how hard would you be willing to work to achieve this? If this is the case, why don't more agents make as much money as doctors?

There is one big difference between pursuing a medical career and one as a real estate agent. The path to success in medicine is highly structured, while the path to success in real estate is not. My question to you is this, If you're staring at the possibility of having a job better than that of a surgeon, in much less time and for much less debt, with the ability to scale yourself out of the business and a better lifestyle while doing it, could you commit yourself to the process with the same vigor and commitment as a medical school student does?

If you can overcome the lack of structure in this profession and find a way to create it for yourself, you will have overcome the biggest barrier to success in our business. Therefore, focus on structuring your day in a way that prioritizes sustained focus on the activities that have the greatest potential to generate income. If you approach this business with the tenacity of a medical student, you can have a much better career than they will!

# Whom to Shadow

While this book will no doubt help you get started in real estate sales, there is no way it can possibly teach you everything you need to know. The vast majority of your education will come from someone else, such as a broker, a coach, or a more experienced agent. No matter whom you decide to learn from, make sure to choose your teachers carefully.

Finding the right person to shadow can catapult you to top-producer status much more quickly than forging a path on your own. My first year in full-time sales got off to a rocky start. My clients looked up to me as a real estate expert, and I felt the pressure to be one. Since I owned more than fifteen rental properties at the time, I believed I knew what I was doing. I absolutely hated it when a client would ask a question I couldn't answer or request information I didn't know how to find. Most of my problems came from not understanding how to perform simple tasks, such as navigating the MLS and filling out a contract efficiently.

I also struggled with *how* to express what I knew I needed to say. Even when I could see the solution to a problem, I desperately needed help articulating it to my clients in a way that wouldn't discourage them. Watching the other agents in my office go about solving problems and listening to them on the phone quickly revealed the difference between those who were struggling just as hard as I was and those who had the confidence I aspired to. One agent, Sedar, stood out among the rest as a great example to me.

Sedar was a straightforward, smart, and experienced agent. She had sold homes for eight years or so and was a top producer every year. I noticed she could play tough when necessary but could also quickly summon her soft side when the situation called for it. Watching Sedar expertly shuttle among clients, agents, emails, and phone calls made me realize I could improve my own game by learning from her. I decided to find how I could bring value to her so that she would want to help me get my new career off to the right start.

One day I heard Sedar admit she hated putting out signs for open houses. Apparently, getting in and out of a car multiple times, then carrying heavy signs around to plant them in the ground during the heat of summer isn't a lot of fun. I offered to meet Sedar at her next open house and put out the signs for her, then come pick them up when she was done. From that point forward, I had my mentor.

Sedar showed me the systems she used to run her business. She taught me that if I wanted to convert a lead, I needed to set an appointment and get in front of them as soon as possible. She showed me how to run open houses, read the other agents, and make sure to listen to both spouses (not just the one who talked more) during a listing appointment.

When choosing your own top producer to shadow, take their personal style into account as well. There are as many ways to succeed in real estate as there are successful agents. Some get by on the strength of their personality, while others take a more numbers-based approach. Some find clients through sheer force of will, while others are savvier at recognizing who they will work best with. If your strength is building authentic relationships but you choose to shadow a door-knocking machine, you could wind up burned out and discouraged.

If you love running open houses, look for those in your office who run them well. If you love to network, connect with agents who go to all the big events and try to tag along. Don't just look for the agent who sells the most houses. You'll learn a lot more by shadowing a top-producing agent whose style aligns with your own—and you'll have a lot more fun doing it too.

## Database Importance

While I've already mentioned the importance of strong database management several times, I want to end on this note because it's the aspect of running a real estate business that will have the greatest impact on your success. Every business has a "funnel," or a process by which resources are converted into revenue. For example, the ability of a farmer to convert seeds to crops will determine how successful the farmer is. I'd like you to consider your real estate business the same way a farmer considers growing crops.

Your database is the fields where you will grow your crops. If you continue planting seeds, watering them, providing the right mix of sun and shade, and weeding as needed, you can expect a great harvest. If you don't, your results will be very inconsistent, which is emotionally frustrating. This affects your degree of effort and commitment, which makes it harder to achieve your goals. If a farmer does a good job raising their crops, they will earn the right to a strong harvest. The harvest is when the farmer is able to take the food they have grown out of the ground and sell it. This is the point in their funnel where they convert their hard work into revenue.

In the world of real estate sales, our crops are people. The way we work those in our database will determine our success in the same way a farmer's success is determined by the way they work their fields. Plant seeds by adding new people to your database. Water your crops by building a relationship with them. Weed your fields by preventing other agents from stealing your leads. Harvest your crops through lead conversion. This is where the people in your database raise their hand and say, "I'm ready to buy/sell a house and I'd like you to help me." This is where all your hard work in tending your database—the fields of your business—pays off.

Getting the harvest right is very important! A farmer who screws up the harvesting of their crops earns no profit from the hard work of growing them. Can you imagine how discouraging that would be? If you had spent six months to a year raising your crops, then lost everything before it could be sold, would you want to start the process over and plant new seed?

For many the answer is no. The impact on your mindset when you fail to convert a lead you have spent a large amount of time and energy developing can be devastating. As I mentioned earlier, maintaining a healthy state of mind is critical. This is why I stress the importance of practicing your presentations and keeping a high conversion rate. Not only will this get you more clients, it will also keep you in a positive frame of mind and keep your business running efficiently.

Running a great database will produce an abundance of leads, just as running a great field will produce an abundance of crops. But can you ensure a successful harvest if you grow more crops than one person can handle before they rot in the fields? As a solo agent, you own a business with no employees. You are akin to a farmer without field hands, which is a recipe for burnout as well as blown leads.

Farmers know they can get more accomplished at harvest with help. One of the best aspects of owning a real estate business is the opportunity to leverage out certain tasks to make sure someone is watering the seeds you planted, pulling the weeds from your field, or making sure the ripe crops are harvested. I learned this early on, implemented it, and watched my fields grow.

## Concluding Thoughts

My goal for this book was to provide all the information I wished someone had given me when I became an agent. I hope you are left feeling more confident, inspired, and driven to work on your craft, improve your ability to represent clients, and thereby increase your earnings. As you apply the principles in this book, you will absolutely see an increase in business and revenue.

While that may seem like your ultimate goal, I want to challenge this thinking. Earning more revenue is good. Building a great business is better. Turning that business into a passive income-generating machine that continues to produce one bountiful harvest after another is best.

Book two in this *Top-Producing Real Estate Agent* series will focus on taking the principles you've learned in this book and helping you expand upon them to create not just a successful business, but a massively successful one. You will learn how to become a "mega agent," earning three to four times as much as the average agent but without working even a single hour more (and avoiding the majority of the tasks involved in your business that drain you the most). As you master the concepts in this book and reach a new "capacity," you will start the process of the Four C's again. You will incorporate new tactics, strategies, and models to help you start a new iteration of your business's growth cycle, making your business even better.

Book three in the series will teach you how to take this new, high-powered machine you've built and work your way out of the business entirely. By the time you're done, you will have complete autonomy and the capacity to choose which roles you'd like to play in the business—or whether you want to play any role all. This is when you achieve truly passive income, like the farmer who owns the fields and hires others to work them and harvest the crops. Earning a great income for yourself while simultaneously providing a good living, growth opportunities, and strategic partnerships to others helps those you hire to improve their lives as well.

I learned the power of real estate by investing in it myself. In my book *Buy, Rehab, Rent, Refinance, Repeat: The BRRRR Rental Property Investment Strategy Made Simple* I likened the power of investing in real estate to surfing a wave. It can catch you and carry you way farther than you ever could have gone by just swimming alone.

This is true of real estate sales as well. I recommend you find a friend, partner, or associate in the office and practice the scripts, tools, and strategies you've read here. Practice them over and over until they feel effortless, not stressful, and your anxiety is replaced by excitement. Focus most intently on the most important pieces of the business, such as lead generation, relationship-building, learning from the best, etc.

Finally, remember your Big Why. Remind yourself daily of your main reason for doing this, who you are doing it for, and why it's so important. The entrepreneur Jim Rohn is credited with saying "Your level of success will rarely exceed your level of personal development," and I have found this to be true. If you want to build a big business, you must become a better person first. And if you keep your Big Why at top of mind at all times, you'll be constantly driven to accomplish personal development sooner.

If you've committed to improving the performance of your business, commit also to continual growth to be the best you can be. The power of real estate will reward you if you do! I hope you've enjoyed this book and turn back to it time and time again when you feel stuck or need answers to questions no one else has been providing. Now get out there and put some people through your funnel!

# ➡ KEY CHAPTER POINTS

- *How* you say and do things is more important to clients than *what* you actually do.
- Lessons you have learned earlier in life can be applicable to your real estate career, and lessons you learn in this phase of your career can help you in the next.
- The Four C's are commitment, courage, capability, and capacity. They represent the cycle you go through to achieve success in your endeavors.
- Failure is a crucial ingredient in the recipe of success. To avoid failure is to avoid success.
- Top-producing agents can make more money than a typical doctor without the massive debt or the eleven- to fifteen-year time commitment they must make before they begin earning money.
- A huge benefit to the business of real estate sales is the ability to scale and leverage. Failing to take advantage of this fact is short-changing yourself and making your job harder than it needs to be.
- Most agents struggle with lack of structure. If you can provide the structure you're lacking, you have overcome a huge obstacle in your path to financial success.

- Finding the right agent to shadow can be a big benefit to your career.
- Top producers are the best agents to shadow. Choose a top producer with a personality or business model you'd like to emulate and look for creative ways to add value for them.
- Your database is extremely important. It is of the same importance as a field is to a farmer.
- As you master the principles in this book, look for ways to step up your business and make more money without expending more effort.
- The ultimate goal of the business owner is to produce passive income. This is possible with real estate sales. If you continue growing through each new cycle of the Four C's, you can turn your job into a business and your business into passive income.
- Improvements in technology have made the transition of real estate sales from a local enterprise to a virtual one even more possible. The dream of working from the beach and making money on vacation is entirely possible if you create the right systems and hire the right people.
- Be sure to connect with me on BiggerPockets.com—I'm a Premium member and would love to meet you!

# ACKNOWLEDGMENTS

This book is dedicated to my first assistant and the bedrock of my company, Krista Keller. Thank you, Krista, for sticking by my side and growing what we have together. There's zero chance I could have done this without you, and I thank God for your presence.

I'd also like to thank Kyle Renke for trusting me enough to make the jump and follow me into the unknown to forge a path I hope many will eventually follow. You did a good job helping edit the book, and a great job serving our clients and building our systems.

I am grateful to David Osborn for introducing me to Keller Williams and getting me started, Jay Papasan for the guidance he provides both directly and indirectly, Gary Keller for teaching agents how to build a business from a job, and Daniel Del Real for providing the perfect example of what an agent should be.

Thank you to Katie Miller for believing in this book, and to Tim Klotz for your continued mentorship, support, and guidance.

I'd also like to thank Kaylee Pratt for marketing, Wendy Dunning for the design, Louise Collazo for editing, and Katie Golownia for proofreading.

Finally, I'd like to thank every single client who ever bought or sold with me. You trusted me with one of the biggest decisions you'll ever make and believed in me enough to help me get this plane off the ground and into the sky. I learned these lessons on your behalf, and none of it would have happened without you!

# BiggerPocketsPremium

## Join now and...

- **Grow your business** with the most qualified investor leads in the industry

- Build an enhanced company profile, lead capture form, promoted status in company directories, and more **for $99/month**.

- Start tapping into BiggerPockets' **rapidly growing network** of motivated real estate investors with...

  — **Over 1.6 million members**

  — **2.1 million monthly visitors**

  — **10B in annual transaction volume**

# Testimonials

"BiggerPockets members made up 40% of my clients in 2019. Our membership is by far our highest performing lead source from an ROI perspective."

**—Jon Bombaci, Premium Agent**

"Over 80% of the leads I connect with using Premium convert to clients."

**—Jake Fugman, Premium Agent**

"I have been able to close 80-85% of the leads I received, and they have been overwhelmingly positive and engaging."

**—Lien Voung, Premium Agent**

Use the code:
# PREMIUMAGENT
for 20% off the lifetime of your membership.

# More from
# BiggerPockets Publishing

### *Set for Life: Dominate Life, Money, and the American Dream*

Looking for a plan to achieve financial freedom in just five to ten years? *Set for Life* by BiggerPockets CEO Scott Trench is a detailed fiscal plan targeted at the average-income earner starting with few or no assets. It will walk you through three stages of finance, guiding you to your first $25,000 in tangible net worth, then to your first $100,000, and then to financial freedom. *Set for Life* will teach you how to build a lifestyle, career, and investment portfolio capable of supporting financial freedom to let you live the life of your dreams.

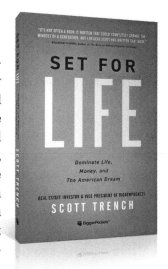

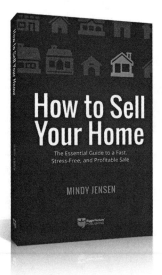

### *How to Sell Your Home*

Selling a home involves far more than sticking a "For Sale" sign in the yard. The stakes are much higher, since a single mistake can cost you thousands of dollars and months of stress. Author Mindy Jensen gives pages of practical, real-world advice to get your house sold for top dollar. Don't leave the biggest sale of your life to chance!

If you enjoyed this book, we hope you'll take a moment to check out some of the other great material BiggerPockets offers. BiggerPockets is the real estate investing social network, marketplace, and information hub, designed to help make you a smarter real estate investor through podcasts, books, blog posts, videos, forums, and more. Sign up today—it's free! **Visit www.BiggerPockets.com.**

---

### *The House Hacking Strategy*

Don't pay for your home. Hack it and live for free! When mastered, house hacking can save you thousands of dollars in monthly expenses, build tens of thousands of dollars in equity each year, and provide the financial means to retire early. Discover why so many successful investors support their investment careers with house hacking—and learn from a frugality expert who has hacked his way toward financial freedom.

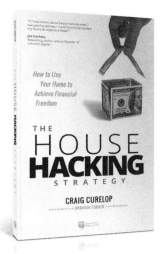

### *How to Invest in Real Estate*

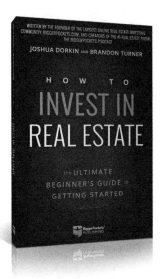

Two of the biggest names in the real estate world teamed up to put together the most comprehensive manual ever written on getting started in the lucrative business of real estate investing. Joshua Dorkin and Brandon Turner give you an insider's look at the many different real estate niches and strategies so that you can find the one that works best for you, your resources, and your goals.

# CONNECT WITH BIGGERPOCKETS

## and Become Successful in Your Real Estate Business Today!

Facebook
/BiggerPockets

Instagram
@BiggerPockets

Twitter
@BiggerPockets

LinkedIn
/company/Bigger
Pockets

Website
BiggerPockets.com